SELLCHOLOGY

SELLCHOLOGY

THE KEY TO HUMAN DRIVE AND DECISION

Ariel Feder

A.K.F. Publishing Company

To the most profound person I know, my daughter Keila.

To the most astute person I know, my daughter Nessa.

To my true love, Yulya, the most radiant person I know.

You taught me love, companionship, and family.

Contents

Introduction

You are reading this because you want to master the complex art of sales—or perhaps to train others to do the same. Either way, I value your time, and I intend to make this worth it.

You already know the "classic" sales world. Management demands that every opportunity be dutifully logged in Salesforce to measure funnel creation and conversion rates. Alongside Marketing, you feed the machine: generating leads, qualifying prospects, and moving them through the pipeline.

At some point, your company sent you to methodology training—Miller Heiman, MEDDIC, or something similar. You learned to build account plans, map org charts, identify stakeholders, and hunt for the elusive Champion.

Then comes the annual sales summit—whether your company calls it SKO, Sales Enablement, or Sales University. Product managers hype the latest features. VPs preach value selling, pipeline discipline, and the eternal mantra: "Close without discounting."

Back in the field, you execute. You identify needs, validate pain points, and craft the perfect value proposition. You follow the process to the letter.

And yet, you know the quiet truth: these methodologies do not turn a good salesperson into a great one.

Why?

Because deep down, you know what you are actually dealing with: complex human beings. People driven by inspiration, fears, hopes, and dreams. Customers—like all humans—make impulsive, emotional, and seemingly irrational decisions at the eleventh hour.

You have seen it happen. You invest in a six-month evaluation, execute flawlessly, and demonstrate undeniable ROI—only to watch the customer stick with the status quo to avoid risk. Or they decide to build an internal solution that could easily be bought from you—not because it makes financial sense, but because it feels safer—or more prestigious.

The salespeople who thrive in this complexity—the ones who read human psychology in real time—are the ones we call truly great. They don't win deals because they keep a cleaner CRM. They win because they understand the invisible forces driving the person sitting across from them. They possess the empathy to sense what a customer feels and the intuition to know precisely what to do next. They have mastered the human element.

And yet, traditional sales training entirely ignores psychology. It focuses on process, org charts, and discount thresholds—necessary tools, but wildly insufficient for winning complex, high-stakes sales.

Why? Because human psychology is inherently resistant to rigid frameworks.

Translating academic psychological theory into a practical, daily methodology is profoundly difficult. Human behavior is messy. Theories often contradict one another, sounding brilliant in a lecture hall but proving utterly useless in a boardroom when the pressure is on and the deal is on the line. In those high-stakes moments, you rely almost entirely on empathy to connect and intuition to steer. The magical combination of those two traits is the trademark of a master seller.

This begs the question: Are we left with, "You either have it or you don't"? Must you simply be born with the "gift" of intuition, or does a learnable framework exist?

I refuse to accept that it is purely innate. A learnable framework does exist.

Yes, every buyer is different. But all human beings are driven by the same underlying psychological engines. Across cultures and centuries, we have developed identical social instincts. We all seek belonging. We all desire purpose. And we all deeply fear losing what we already possess.

Because of this shared human condition, we can define a psychology-based sales methodology—one that actively decodes human drive. It is a framework designed to take us from good to great.

This is exactly why I wrote *Sellchology*.

The goal is not merely to philosophize about human nature, but to answer the most fundamental questions in business:

What ultimately drives someone to make a decision and act?

How do you inspire someone to take a risk, sign a contract, or champion a cause—and genuinely feel grateful for the opportunity?

How are decisions truly formed in the quiet, invisible spaces of the human mind, long before they become words in a meeting or a signature on a page?

In this book, we will construct that framework using three powerful pillars, born from the brightest minds and darkest moments of the 20th century:

- Inspiration (Viktor Frankl): Forged in the concentration camps of World War II to provide ultimate meaning and purpose.

- Motivation (Abraham Maslow): Offering a structural path to personal and professional fulfillment.

- Persuasion (Daniel Kahneman): Utilizing behavioral economics to actively drive and frame decisions.

By mastering this architecture, you will learn to anchor your solution in your customer's future, fulfill their deepest psychological needs, and make choosing you feel natural—almost inevitable.

This methodology is heavily grounded in the work of the greatest psychological minds of the last century. Yet, it is far from academic theory. It has been forged, refined, and battle-tested in the unforgiving arena of global, high-stakes enterprise tech sales.

> **If I have seen further, it is by standing on the shoulders of giants.[1]**
>
> — *Isaac Newton*

CHAPTER 1

Inspiration

He who has a why to live can bear almost any how.[2]

— Friedrich Nietzsche

The single most powerful human drive is Inspiration.

Inspiration operates entirely outside the standard calculus of gain and loss. It is a spiritual, transcendental force that drives us to action based on a profound sense of belief and meaning. Since the dawn of civilization, humanity has recognized inspiration as our highest calling—a truth echoed across ancient religious and philosophical texts.

To understand its power, we must look at its origins. The word inspiration comes from the Latin *inspirare*, meaning "to breathe into." It was originally used to describe a divine or supernatural force entering the body to animate, guide, or stir the soul. In classical Latin and early Christian texts, inspiration was understood as a holy drive—a higher power infusing life, purpose, and revelation into a human being.

This sacred notion is beautifully captured in the Book of Genesis, where God "breathed into" the nostrils of the man He had formed from dust, transforming him into a living soul:

"And the Lord God formed man of the dust of the ground, and breathed into his nostrils the breath of life; and man became a living soul."
— Genesis 2:7[3]

We see the sheer force of this drive in the Talmudic story of Rabbi Akiva, one of Judaism's greatest sages. Executed by the Romans in the second century CE for defying their laws, Akiva was subjected to unimaginable torture. Yet, as the Romans tore his flesh with iron combs, he calmly recited the Shema Yisrael prayer[4], affirming the oneness of God.

Horrified, his students asked him, "Our teacher, even now?"

Rabbi Akiva replied, "All my life I have wondered about the verse, 'You shall love the Lord your God... with all your soul'—even if He takes your soul. Now that I have the chance to fulfill it, should I not?"[5]

Rabbi Akiva did not act out of obligation or fear. He was moved by a spiritual inspiration so absolute that even in the face of agonizing death, he made a conscious, faithful choice. Like other accounts of religious martyrs, his story represents the pinnacle of devotion: the moment where inspiration outweighs primal fear, and meaning overcomes suffering.

We find this exact philosophical struggle in the oldest written story ever discovered: *The Epic of Gilgamesh*. Dating back over 4,000 years to ancient Mesopotamia, it tells the tale of Gilgamesh, king of Uruk, who is devastated by the death of his closest companion, Enkidu. Grief-stricken and terrified by the realization of his own mortality, he sets out on a desperate quest for eternal life.

At this point in the epic, his motivation is not spiritual; it is deeply personal and driven entirely by fear:

"Must I die too? Must I be as Enkidu? Sorrow has entered my heart. I am afraid of death, so I roam over the steppe."[6]

Gilgamesh ultimately fails in his quest. Because his pursuit of immortality is rooted in the primal need to survive rather than the pursuit of meaning, he is simply trying to outrun death.

But then, something shifts. Returning to Uruk empty-handed, Gilgamesh begins to view his life through a different lens. He turns his focus away from escaping death and toward building something that will outlast him—a permanent legacy for his people.

This is the turning point: fear gives way to inspiration. He begins acting not for his own survival, but for a purpose greater than himself.

"Go up on the wall of Uruk and walk around. Inspect the foundation terrace and examine the brickwork: is not its brickwork of burnt brick? And did not the seven sages lay its foundations?"[7]

The ancient Akkadians left us a lesson that remains profoundly true today: when we chase meaning rather than escape, and when we act out of inspiration rather than fear, we awaken to our true purpose. A higher goal—one that reaches beyond ourselves—is not just stronger than the fear of death. It is the very thing that gives life its meaning.

These stories prove that inspiration is fundamentally hardwired into our human nature. Across time and cultures, the pattern holds true: when people act from deep inspiration—rather than fear or transactional desire—they find purpose, meaning, and the strength to rise above their limitations.

It is the strongest drive we possess. It moves us far more than the promise of personal gain, or the threat of loss.

Where do we feel this ancient force today?

Parenthood

Consider how parenthood redefines the very essence of meaning. From the moment it begins—with pain, sleepless nights, and what feels like a never-ending mountain of diapers—it transforms everything. Parenthood inspires a shift in priorities like nothing else can. Suddenly, you find yourself neglecting your own needs—goodbye, hot meals and uninterrupted Netflix binges—for the sake of a little person who depends entirely on you. It's hard, it's messy, and it never stops.

Yet amid the chaos, a profound sense of purpose emerges. Watching your child take their first steps, succeed at their dreams, or reflect your values makes it all worthwhile. We often view parenthood as one of life's greatest achievements, and for good reason: the relationship you build with your child becomes the most important and enduring connection in your life. It's this relentless inspiration to nurture, protect, and guide that turns even the toughest moments into a legacy of love and fulfillment. And let's be honest—who else but your kids could inspire you to function on two hours of sleep and still show up with snacks?

Love

Do you remember that feeling—the butterflies in your belly, the rush of your heart racing faster than your thoughts, and the sudden inability to speak coherently around someone who made the world stop spinning? In those early years, love felt electric—didn't it? It wasn't just an emotion; it was an adventure, a mystery, a spark that set your entire being alight. You'd spend hours dissecting a glance or replaying a conversation in your mind, wondering if they felt it too. That first rush of love had a way of making everything feel bigger, brighter, and more meaningful, as if the world existed just for the two of you. It inspired you to take risks you never thought you'd take—passing notes in class, waiting hours by the phone, or pouring your heart into a song, poem, or text message. And while love has a way of evolving, there's something magical about that first dance with it—the giddy excitement, the nervous anticipation, and the belief that anything was possible. Those butterflies? They weren't just in your belly—they were the wings of inspiration, lifting you into a world where love made everything feel infinite.

Faith

Faith, as Yuval Noah Harari discusses in *Sapiens*, is one of humanity's most powerful tools for creating shared purpose and driving progress. Harari explains that faith—whether in gods, nations, or ideas—has inspired humans to unite in pursuit of common goals, enabling them to build civilizations, craft laws, and trust in unseen possibilities. This kind of shared belief has been the foundation of cooperation and innovation, transforming scattered groups into powerful, collective forces. Faith inspires individuals and societies to strive for something beyond themselves—even when the outcome is uncertain. Faith is not only about belief—it is about the inspiration to act, to create, and to move forward together.[8]

Inspiration is stronger than Motivation

At its root, inspiration is a direct path to self-actualization and transcendence. Inspiration is not about fulfilling the need for food, shelter, or esteem. Those needs drive us to act through motivation, as we will explore in the next chapter. Inspiration, however, leads us to transcendence despite the unfulfilled needs. It drives us to act not for personal gain but to create something beyond ourselves. Something that holds meaning for us on a spiritual level or supports our core beliefs. In many cases, the drive of Inspiration leads us to sacrifice—the exact opposite of Motivation. We are driven to lose rather than gain, yet we remain driven.

One of the most influential books ever written, *Man's Search for Meaning* (1946), captures the power of inspiration through Viktor Frankl's experiences in Nazi concentration camps during World War II. More than a memoir, it reveals how meaning sustains the human spirit even in the darkest times, making it a cornerstone of existential thought.

Viktor Frankl (1905–1997) was an Austrian neurologist, psychiatrist, and Holocaust survivor best known as the founder of Logotherapy, a psychological approach centered on finding meaning in life. His seminal work, *Man's Search for Meaning*, is a foundational text in existential psychology, where he argues that the primary human drive is not pleasure (Freud), superiority (Adler), or fulfilling needs (Maslow), but rather the pursuit of meaning. Frankl observed that even in the harshest conditions—such as World War II concentration camps—those who had a sense of purpose, a *why* to live for, could endure unimaginable suffering. He famously quoted Nietzsche:

"He who has a Why to live can bear almost any how."[9]

— *Friedrich Nietzsche*

This profound insight forms the basis of Logotherapy, emphasizing that meaning is not just a luxury for those whose needs are met but a fundamental force that drives human resilience, inspiration, and survival. Viktor Frankl's existential psychology is the cornerstone of this view of inspiration, meaning, and faith. By understanding Viktor Frankl's approach to the treatment of the human soul, we will understand how to use inspiration in sales.

But why Frankl?

What sets Frankl apart—and makes his ideas so valuable to us—is that he lived what he taught. His theories weren't just academic. They were forged in the hardest conditions imaginable: in concentration camps, where he tested them on himself. Later, he refined them through decades of real-world clinical work.

After World War II, Viktor Frankl returned to Vienna and led the neurology department at the General Polyclinic Hospital for 25 years. He also treated patients in his private practice for about 35 years, up until his retirement in 1970.

Beyond his clinical work, Frankl dedicated his life to teaching and writing about existential psychology and logotherapy. He served as a professor at the University of Vienna until the age of 85 and held visiting positions at Harvard, Stanford, and other top institutions.[10]

Unlike theorists such as B.F. Skinner, who stayed mostly in the lab, or Nietzsche, who observed life from a philosophical distance, Frankl was a practitioner. Like you and me, he was in it. That's why we can trust him. His insights are grounded in experience.

Three Paths to Meaning and Inspiration by Viktor Frankl

Viktor Frankl introduced the concept of the "Three Paths to Meaning" in his seminal work, *Man's Search for Meaning* (1946). [11] He outlines three primary ways individuals can discover meaning in life:

The First Way: Creating or Contributing to Something Greater Than Yourself.

People are inspired when they see their efforts contributing to something greater than themselves. Whether through innovation, leadership, or craftsmanship, individuals find meaning in what they create and achieve.

Frankl suggests we uncover meaning by working toward a goal that is greater than ourselves. In a business context, this might happen when an organization has a clear mission that addresses a social need or advances the well-being of a community. Employees who realize that their day-to-day tasks are part of this larger narrative often feel more enthusiastic and committed. Rather than carrying out routines mechanically, they see their contributions as integral to a collective aim that positively impacts the world around them.

As successful sales professionals, we must first understand a company's reason for existence—why it was created and what it truly stands for. Recognizing what drives their organization beyond profit, how they contribute to the world, and the deeper meaning behind their mission is essential. This understanding comes from researching their goals, listening to their narrative, and identifying shared values.

A salesperson must then reflect and find a genuine, personal reason to support the customer—something that cannot be faked. Once this authentic alignment is established, they can present it back to the customer through products and services, not as a sales pitch but as a real, honest effort to help fulfill the company's purpose.

This transforms sales from a transactional exchange into a meaningful partnership, creating alignment beyond profit and loss. It fosters a union of vision and collaboration, built on mutual meaning, inspiring both companies to grow together. Only true alignment is authentic—genuine purpose cannot be faked or manipulated.

The Second Path: Experiencing Someone or Something

Meaning emerges from deep connections with others, from love and shared experiences. By merging with another, we experience something greater than ourselves. We are inspired by the character and beauty of another person. The interaction and deep connection inspire us and give us meaning.

The pursuit of meaning in work is not solely rooted in relationships—it is also found in the labor of love that unites professionals through shared passion and craftsmanship. Engineers are bound by their love for technology, constantly pushing the boundaries of innovation. Business leaders are driven by their love for efficiency, striving to optimize systems and create sustainable impact. Creators, whether designers, developers, or entrepreneurs, find fulfillment in the experience of bringing something new to life, entering a state of flow and self-actualization. This passion transforms work from a mere obligation into a deeply engaging pursuit, where challenges become opportunities for mastery. Inspirational leadership and salesmanship are not only about fostering human connections but also about creating an environment where passion thrives. When people are immersed in meaningful work that aligns with their innate drive for innovation and progress, they experience a profound sense of purpose—one that transcends transactions and fuels genuine, long-term engagement.

The Third Path: Attitude in Suffering

Frankl's most powerful insight is that even in suffering, people can find meaning. Those who face hardship with resilience and purpose often become a source of inspiration—proving that growth, adaptation, and transcendence are possible, even in the darkest moments.

Today's business world is no stranger to suffering. Rapid technological change makes systems obsolete. Regulations shift. The war for talent drains teams. Top performers leave. Competitors poach. Expansion brings complexity. Supply chains break. Customer expectations evolve faster than you can respond. These are not just operational hurdles—they are emotional, cultural, and strategic pains. Companies quietly ask: Can we adapt fast enough? Will we lose ourselves as we grow? Does our vision still matter? Employees feel it in long hours, shifting roles, and limited resources. Leaders face it in difficult trade-offs—layoffs, restructures, constant change. And like individuals, organizations are defined by how they respond to suffering.

This is where the best business partners make a difference. Great salespeople and co-visionaries don't just offer solutions—they share the struggle. They stand with customers in uncertainty, listen deeply, and help carry the load. In times of disruption, trust is earned not through promises, but through presence, empathy, and real partnership.

Just as Frankl taught, suffering isn't something to avoid—it's something to transform. With the right attitude, it becomes a catalyst for clarity, strategy, and renewed purpose.

When life asks us, we must answer.[12]

— *Viktor Frankl*

Inspiration in business partnership

True partnership is not about transactions; it is about Inspiration, Shared Meaning, and Transformation. When we enter a customer's world as outsiders, we behave like merchants: we present features, defend pricing, and compete for budget. But when we step into the customer's struggle as co-visionaries, something changes. The relationship stops being "buyer vs. seller" and becomes "builders of the same future."

This is not romantic language. It is practical. Companies do not endure disruption by purchasing tools. They endure by finding a reason to keep building—by turning pressure into purpose. In the best partnerships, both sides do that work together. The challenges are not only problems to be fixed; they become raw material for reinvention, resilience, and leadership.

The inspirational salespeople don't merely sell to suffering. They stand with it. And that stance creates a bond that is hard to break—because it is built on meaning, not convenience. Together, through innovation, adaptability, and shared resilience, we don't just survive hard seasons. We use them as catalysts for something stronger than what existed before.

The shared struggle

We've seen how individuals can find meaning in suffering. But can a company suffer?

Absolutely. Organizations bleed—just differently. They carry the pain of losing talent, the exhaustion of constant change, and the weight of market shifts. Like Frankl's patients, a company can endure suffering only if it has meaning—a vision worth paying for.

Most salespeople stand outside this suffering, throwing "solutions" over the wall. The inspirational salesperson steps inside. They say, in essence:

"I see the legacy you are trying to build. I'm not here to sell you a tool. I'm here to help carry the load."

In that moment, you stop being a vendor negotiating a price. You become a partner sharing the fate of the mission. You are no longer watching them struggle—you are helping them translate struggle into meaning.

Where do organizations find this meaning?

Inside every customer organization, inspiration is already present—often quietly, often under pressure.

- **Work (Creation / Craft):** Engineers find meaning in building what did not exist before—solving hard problems, pushing boundaries, and improving the world one constraint at a time. Long hours become tolerable when the work feels like creation rather than extraction.

- **Love (Connection / Care):** Managers find purpose in developing people and building teams that can do what individuals cannot. They carry responsibility not just for delivery, but for culture: trust, pride, and belonging. This is love in its professional form—care expressed as leadership.

- **Suffering (Attitude / Resilience):** Leaders and managers face moments that test identity: layoffs, lost deals, lawsuits, and public failures. In these moments, the organization's character is revealed. Suffering forces the question: Who are we when it hurts?

Organizations can find inspiration in all three. Some are born from a visionary mission that attracts talent like gravity. Others mature through a "labor of love"—the discipline of craft, collaboration, and long-term building. And every organization, sooner or later, meets hardship that demands resilience, dignity, and humanity from everyone inside it.

As sales professionals, we can align with our customers and, in a real sense, borrow their meaning. Their inspiration becomes part of ours. We become Co-Visionaries.

Co-Visionaries are hard to replace.

A procurement manager might be tempted by a 10% cost reduction. But when a partnership is tied to mission-critical execution, C-level leadership often protects it. Co-Visionaries who share their values and stand with them in hardship are not replaced lightly. Customers may test alternatives, negotiate hard, and challenge assumptions. Yet they rarely abandon partners who have proven they understand the mission and can carry pressure with them—not for a flashy demo or a mere 10% reduction.

Implementation of Inspiration in Sales.

Let us define a process with clear success criteria to drive the decision of our customers through mutual inspiration and co-vision.

Step One: Discovery of Inspiration.

The first step is to deeply understand what inspires your customer. This begins with learning everything you can about the company and its leadership. Study the company's origin story, core values, and mission statement. Read about the executives—what they believe in, what drives them. Watch interviews, listen to talks, and read articles or blog posts they've written. Their website, social media, press releases, commercials, and customer testimonials all offer valuable insight.

Read about their products and services, and more importantly, the problems they are solving. Understanding how they help their own customers gives you a window into how they seek to fulfill their mission. This is where inspiration lives—in the gap between the problem and the purpose.

But don't stop at online research. As sales professionals, we're privileged to engage with customers directly. Use every interaction—formal and informal—as an opportunity to ask questions, listen closely, and pick up on what truly moves them. Most leaders are eager to share their vision when they feel they're speaking to someone who genuinely cares.

As you already know, leading a company isn't a walk in the park. It's hard, high-pressure work filled with constant challenges. These individuals could easily choose less stressful lives, but they don't. Why? Because they are driven—by a vision, by personal meaning, by a desire to make something better. With enough rapport and real curiosity, they will let you in.

Step Two: Ask Questions.

Leaders are used to sharing their vision. They do it every day—to employees, investors, customers, and yes, suppliers. Your job is to ask thoughtful questions, show real interest, and allow yourself to be infected by their inspiration.

Viktor Frankl in his logotherapy practice asked Socratic Questions to help his patients reveal their meaning in life. Their 'Why'.

We may use Logotherapy framework to understand and extract the life meaning of the company that we would like to do business with. These questions challenge us to reflect deeply, strip away superficial distractions, and commit to our customer's sense of purpose. Applying Viktor Frankl's logotherapy principles to organizations, we will frame Socratic questions to uncover the deeper meaning behind a company's existence.

These questions are precise, sharp, and drive clarity.

Phase 1: Diagnosing the Existential Vacuum (Why Do We Exist?)

1. **"Beyond financial success, what significant problem does your business exist to solve, and why does it matter?"**

A company that exists only to make money is like a person who wakes up every day with no reason to get out of bed. Viktor Frankl argued that people need a purpose to endure hardship, and businesses are no different. The companies that thrive—especially in tough markets—are those that stand for something more than profit. In sales, this is critical. Customers who have a clear, meaningful problem to solve are the ones worth pursuing. They are invested in solutions that drive progress, not just cut costs. If a business sees your offering as a tool to achieve its deeper mission, price becomes secondary. These customers are looking for partners, not vendors, because their success depends on long-term relationships. When you understand their deeper struggle, you're not just another salesperson—you're the one who helps them move forward.

2. **"If your company ceased to exist tomorrow, who—customers, employees, or society—would miss it the most, and why?"**

A business that can disappear without anyone noticing is a business with no real foundation. Frankl wrote that meaning is found in responsibility—who do we matter to? The same applies to companies. A business that is essential—to its customers, employees, or industry—has a built-in advantage. In sales, this means looking for customers who are deeply embedded in their markets, not those who just happen to be making money right now. If their absence would leave a gap, they have long-term potential, and selling to them means investing in stability and future growth. Customers who are essential are looking for suppliers, service providers, and partners who make them even more valuable to their own audience. If you can make them irreplaceable to their customers, you become irreplaceable to them.

3. **"What conventional belief or outdated practice does your company challenge, and why?"**

Every industry has its dinosaurs—companies that keep doing things the way they always have because "that's how it's done." These companies are slow, resistant to change, and often the first to fail when the market shifts. Frankl believed that meaning comes from confronting suffering rather than avoiding it, and in business, that means challenging the status quo instead of accepting it. The best customers in sales are the ones who refuse to play by outdated rules—they are the ones who want to move forward, innovate, and disrupt. These customers aren't looking for the cheapest option; they're looking for a competitive edge. If your product or service helps them break free from industry norms, they will invest in it because it aligns with their mission. Selling to these customers means positioning yourself not just as a provider, but as a key enabler of their transformation.

Phase 2: Connecting Meaning to Action—Bridging Vision and Execution

In Phase 1, we uncovered the existential meaning of the company—why it exists and what deeper purpose it serves beyond financial success. Phase 2 is about aligning their purpose with real-world execution and, more importantly, demonstrating how our product, service, or partnership naturally fits into that journey. A company's mission is only valuable if it drives action. The goal here is to bridge the gap between what they stand for and what they do every day, so they can see how our offering is not just useful but essential to fulfilling their purpose. This is where meaning meets business strategy, and where selling becomes co-creating.

4. "What are the critical areas where your company must execute flawlessly to stay true to its purpose?"

This question helps them identify those pressure points, and once they do, we position our solution as a reinforcement, not a disruption. The key here is to help them realize that execution is not just about efficiency or optimization—it's about protecting their core identity. If they fail in these areas, they don't just lose revenue; they compromise their credibility, dilute their brand, and weaken their impact. When the stakes are this high, every decision matters. If our product fortifies what makes them who they are, it's not a nice-to-have—it's a strategic necessity for keeping their mission intact and moving forward with confidence. Our products and services are not just tools—they are the infrastructure that supports the execution of their meaning. We don't just help them operate; we help them stay true to their "Why." Every process we strengthen, every system we enhance, is another layer of protection for the purpose they built their business on. This is not about adding value—it's about ensuring that their value is consistently realized, experienced, and never compromised. Our product directly supports their mission, making it a necessary investment in their "Why," not just another expense.

5. "Where do you see the biggest gaps between your company's purpose and its current execution?"

Even the best companies experience a gap between their mission and their reality. Maybe they believe in innovation, but they're using outdated systems. Maybe they stand for quality, but their processes don't fully support it. The point is not to expose flaws—it's to help them see what's already holding them back. Once they acknowledge this, they are primed for a solution. If we present our product as a bridge between their mission and execution, it removes the feeling of being "sold to" and makes the next step obvious and natural. Our products help them bridge the gap to their purpose.

6. "How does innovation play a role in making your company's vision a reality?"

In Phase 1, we asked the customer, "What conventional belief or outdated practice does your company challenge, and why?" But challenging convention is not just a mindset—it demands action. A company cannot break industry norms or redefine standards by doing things the same way they've always been done. To truly disrupt, they must embrace innovation, whether by leveraging the latest technology, dramatically improving existing processes, or adopting entirely new ways of thinking. This is where our products and services come into play—not as mere tools, but as the enablers of their transformation. Vision alone is wishful thinking unless it is backed by innovation. This question forces the customer to confront the necessity of innovation.

Summary Question:

"How can we improve to better bring your company's mission to life?"

From my experience, a business is not built just by getting the customer excited about something. Enthusiasm fades quickly when they step into internal meetings, face resistance from colleagues, or encounter the real challenges of implementing change. A strong pitch may spark interest, but it does not guarantee action.

The real purpose of this question is to understand how the customer sees our partnership—not just in theory, but in real execution. More importantly, it helps us uncover the roadblocks and objections they will inevitably face when trying to integrate our solution. These objections are not just personal concerns; they are the collective hesitations of their organization, the challenges that will surface when they attempt to justify the investment, implement the change, or disrupt existing processes.

The worst mistake is to let these objections surface after the meeting, in an email or a follow-up call when the momentum has already faded. By that point, we are just another vendor waiting for a response. Instead, we must address these concerns while we are still in the room, when the energy is high, and when the customer is planning to use our products to reach their vision.

Why does this matter? Because by asking the questions in Phase 1 and Phase 2, we have already demonstrated co-vision. We have positioned ourselves as aligned with their mission, not just selling a product. At this moment, the customer is in a state of trust, inspiration, and belief. They see us as partners in their journey, not outsiders pushing a sale. This is the perfect time to surface and address their biggest concerns about implementing our solution.

Objections do not disappear—they just shift to a place where we are no longer there to respond. If we bring them to light while the customer is still engaged, still open, still in the mindset of transformation, we have the best chance to resolve them, reposition them, and move forward together.

Ending the Meeting: Commitment and Last Impression

After tackling objections and brainstorming solutions, the final step is to solidify alignment and create momentum. A well-structured summary ensures that the conversation doesn't fade into uncertainty once the meeting ends. Start by clearly restating what was agreed upon—this reinforces progress and confirms shared understanding. Next, outline any open tasks, defining who is responsible for what and setting clear ownership. Finally, lock in timing for the next steps, making sure there's a structured path forward rather than an ambiguous follow-up.

However, the emotional conclusion is critical. Always end on a high, optimistic note, bringing the conversation back to the inspiration and co-vision that fueled the discussion.

Why does this matter?

- It strengthens trust and deepens alignment. The customer must walk away with the certainty that we don't just understand their needs—we understand their purpose. They should feel that we aren't just selling to them; we are invested in their mission.

- It shapes the memory of the meeting. Psychologically, people remember the ending of an experience more vividly than the details in between. By closing with energy, inspiration, and excitement about what's ahead, we ensure that when they reflect on this conversation, they associate it with clarity, confidence, and momentum.

This final moment is about securing both logical agreement and emotional buy-in. When the customer leaves, they shouldn't just know that this partnership makes sense—they should feel it.

We will dive deeper into this psychological effect in Chapter 3, where we explore presentation strategies and cognitive biases that influence decision-making. For now, what matters is this: A great meeting is not just one that goes well; it is one that stays with them long after it ends.

Do You Truly Understand Your Customer's Inspiration?

How do you know that you and your sales team are on the right track in understanding and creating drive through inspiration?

The best way to achieve this is by preparing a sales presentation about the customer's actual products. If we, as sales professionals, can successfully pitch and sell our customer's products, it means we have grasped their value proposition. This exercise will naturally lead to questions about the benefits and completeness of our customer's solutions that we can then discuss with them to gain deeper insights. This not only enhances our understanding of their products but also demonstrates genuine interest in their efforts, strengthening our relationship with the customer's engineers.

To refine this presentation, we can deliver it to our internal sales team, application engineers, and customer success.

Next, we should apply the same approach to the customer's company as a whole. By preparing a sales presentation aimed at potential shareholders, we showcase our understanding of the customer's vision and goals. Presenting this to our own managers can help position the customer as a strategic account. Strategic customers receive better pricing and greater focus from both pre-sales and post-sales teams.

These presentations serve as excellent preparation for upcoming campaigns and negotiations. They enable us to speak the customer's language, connect with their vision, and ultimately craft presentations of our own offerings in a way that resonates with their mission and values. These are not just exercises; they are clear signs that we are moving in the right direction.

Summary: The Inspiration Workflow

In this chapter, we saw how inspiration transcends personal gain and connects individuals and organizations to something larger than themselves. Whether drawn from faith, love, craftsmanship, or struggle, inspiration transforms ordinary effort into meaningful action.

In business and sales, inspiration is the foundation of true partnership. When we understand what drives our customers beyond profit, when we connect with their "why," and when our own purpose aligns with theirs, selling becomes something nobler: a shared mission. This workflow turns philosophy into a practical, repeatable process that any professional can use to lead conversations, discover meaning, and co-create vision with customers.

Step One – Discovery of Inspiration

Research deeply to prepare.

1. Study the company's history, vision, and values.

2. Review leadership backgrounds, interviews, letters to shareholders, and press releases.

3. Identify the problem they exist to solve—and the belief that fuels them.

Step Two – Ask Meaningful Questions

Engage with curiosity and empathy. Use the two-phase questioning model inspired by Viktor Frankl to align vision and drive action.

Phase 1: Diagnosing the Existential Vacuum — "Why Do We Exist?"

1. Beyond financial success, what significant problem does your business exist to solve, and why does it matter?

2. If your company ceased to exist tomorrow, who—customers, employees, or society—would miss it most, and why?

3. What conventional belief or outdated practice does your company challenge, and why?

Phase 2: Connecting Meaning to Action — Bridging Vision and Execution

1. What are the critical areas where your company must execute flawlessly to stay true to its purpose?

2. Where do you see the biggest gaps between your company's purpose and its current execution?

3. How does innovation play a role in turning your company's vision into reality?

Step Three – Validation Through the Customer's Lens

Prepare two internal presentations:

1. Pitch the Product: Deliver a sales presentation of the customer's own products and services—to prove you understand their value.

2. Pitch the Vision: Present to your managers—to show you grasp their larger vision and market meaning.

Step Four – Present Your Offering to the Customer

Enter as a partner, not a vendor.

1. Demonstrate sincere alignment with the customer's purpose and mission.

2. Present your products and services as enablers of that mission.

3. Ask: "How can we better bring your company's mission to life?"

4. Listen carefully, gather feedback, and address objections openly and constructively.

In the words of Viktor Frankl:

"Don't aim at success—the more you aim at it and make it a target, the more you are going to miss it. For success, like happiness, cannot be pursued; it must ensue, and it only does so as the unintended side-effect of one's personal dedication to a cause greater than oneself or as the by-product of one's surrender to a person other than oneself."

— Viktor E. Frankl, Man's Search for Meaning[13]

CHAPTER 2

Motivation

Abe felt like a mistake.

Growing up in the crowded, gray streets of Brooklyn, he felt lonely and hunted. As a Jewish boy in a neighborhood where he didn't belong, he learned to keep his head down. He was always listening for the sound of rocks hitting the ground or the ugly insult "kike" shouted by the local boys. It was a cruel word used against Jews to remind him he wasn't welcome.[14]

But the streets were safer than his own home.

Home wasn't a shelter. His father, Samuel, was a rough, drinking man who drifted in and out of the family's life. When home, Samuel would stare at his son's scrawny frame and ask the room, "Have you ever seen anyone so ugly?"[15] Abe believed him. He looked in the mirror and saw what his father saw: a scrawny, grotesque thing, unworthy of love.

But the true source of his existential crisis was his mother, Rose. She was a deeply superstitious and cruel woman who painted the world in terms of punishment. One of Abe's darkest memories—the one that haunted his understanding of human nature—happened when he brought two stray kittens home. He had found them shivering in the street and, desperate for something to love, hid them in the basement, feeding them milk from his own bowl.

When his mother heard their meowing, she did not merely discipline him. In a rage, she grabbed the kittens and smashed their heads against the wall until they were dead. Abe watched, paralyzed. He learned then that the person who was supposed to protect life could also destroy it without remorse.[16]

That night, an existential question emerged in his mind: Why do people choose to be cruel?

He couldn't find the answer at home, so he turned to books. The public library became his cathedral. He would arrive before the doors opened, sitting on the steps, waiting to be let into the only world that made sense. Between the stacks of books, surrounded by the great thinkers, Abe stopped being the ugly boy from Brooklyn. There he discovered the non-religious spirituality of Baruch Spinoza. He saw himself in the outcast hero of the novel *Odd John*. Inspired by the utopian visions of H.G. Wells, he began to dream of a better society—one his own ideas might help build. This childhood forged Abraham Maslow.

His early research at Columbia and Brooklyn College was driven by this very question. Working with primatologist Harry Harlow, he found that once monkeys' basic needs for food and safety were met, they sought contact and affection—a simple but profound hint that motivation moved in layers.

Later, teaching during the Second World War, he watched brilliant students lose confidence under fear and regain it through encouragement and belonging. The pattern repeated itself: from need to safety to esteem to purpose. Maslow began to see what centuries of philosophers had only intuited: that the great theories of motivation were not contradictory but nested.

Maslow was well-versed in the leading psychological findings of his time. Yet, he believed psychology should explain not only what breaks us but also what builds us—the conditions under which ordinary people become capable, generous, even extraordinary. "Freud gave us the sick half of psychology," Maslow later said, "we must now fill in the healthy half."[17]

In 1943, he gathered these insights into his paper "A Theory of Human Motivation" published in Psychological Review.[18] He proposed that human needs are arranged in a hierarchy, beginning with the physiological and ascending through safety, love and belonging, esteem, and finally to what he called self-actualization—the desire "to become everything one is capable of becoming."

For the first time, the scattered intuitions of history formed a single psychological map.

The Philosophers Were Right

Maslow's genius lay not in discovering new human needs, but in seeing the hidden order that connected them. He realized that the great thinkers of history were all right; they had only seen part of the picture. Each philosopher or leader had emphasized a single need, capturing just one aspect of the human soul:

The foundation is physical. Before we can dream or love, we must survive. Like many others before him, Napoleon Bonaparte famously declared, "An army marches on its stomach."[19] No amount of leadership or vision matters if the basic biological machinery is starving.

Thomas Hobbes captured the primal truth that safety and security are the main needs of humans. In his book *Leviathan*, he wrote that life without order is "solitary, poor, nasty, brutish, and short."[20]

We all hope love changes the world. As the Greek philosopher Epicurus stated: "Of all the things which wisdom provides to make life entirely happy, much the greatest is the possession of friendship."[21]

By contrast psychologist Alfred Adler suggested that humans are driven by a need to overcome feelings of inferiority. We do not just want to be liked; we want to be capable. We strive for mastery and recognition to prove that our existence has weight and value.[22]

At the peak, the Drive turns inward. It is no longer about what the world gives us, but what we become. The Buddha taught that true fulfillment comes only when one realizes their unique purpose. In the *Dhammapada*, he warned: "Do not give up your own purpose for the sake of another's... After realizing your own true purpose, devote yourself to it."[23]

Maslow saw that these thinkers were not contradicting each other; they were simply speaking from different altitudes. By stacking these insights, Maslow transformed a centuries-old philosophical debate into a psychological map. He showed that we are not defined by a single drive, but by a dynamic ascent from survival to meaning.

The Hierarchy of Needs

When Maslow published "*A Theory of Human Motivation*" in *Psychological Review*, the world was deep in war, yet his paper opened not with despair, but with faith: "Human behavior is not merely a response to the environment but an expression of inner needs."[24] It was a simple sentence—and a revolution. It suggested that human beings are not passive creatures shaped by circumstance, but self-organizing systems guided by desire, meaning, and possibility.

Maslow outlined five great families of need, woven through every human life. At the foundation stand the physiological needs—air, water, rest, food, warmth. When they are unmet, they consume the mind completely. As he wrote, "A man who is extremely hungry has no other interest but food." But once these are met, even briefly, consciousness expands—new hungers appear, less physical, more human.

The next layer is safety—the craving for order, predictability, and protection from chaos. Children seek it in routines, adults in stability and law. Maslow observed that people will often "prefer a job with some security to one with greater income but more hazard." When the world feels unstable, even the free choose fences.

Then comes the need for love and belonging—the emotional gravity that draws us into families, friendships, teams, and communities. Maslow saw affection not as decoration but as nourishment. Those deprived of it, he wrote, "will hunger for relations with others—for friends, a sweetheart, children, or community." Isolation, to him, was not emptiness—it was deprivation.

From that foundation grows esteem—the need to feel capable, respected, worthy. Maslow distinguished between two kinds: the lower need for recognition by others, and the higher need for confidence earned through mastery. When this need is met, people feel useful and competent; when it's denied, they shrink under inferiority and doubt. A healthy society, he wrote, is one that "permits its members to earn esteem."

And finally, above them all, stands self-actualization—"the desire to become everything one is capable of becoming." Not success, not perfection, but wholeness: the realization of one's potential through expression, creation, contribution. For Maslow, this was not luxury. It was the natural direction of life itself—growth reaching toward its form, like a tree bending toward light.

It was elegant and simple. Yet, it is often misunderstood. Maslow never meant for his hierarchy to be a pyramid.

He warned: "In actual life, this ordering is not nearly so clear-cut as it sounds. All the needs are always present, though in different degrees of relative strength" (Maslow, 1943, p. 383). Human needs are not steps to climb, but waves that rise and recede. Hunger may dull affection, fear may silence creativity, but none disappear. Life is not linear. It oscillates—between safety and adventure, belonging and freedom, self-doubt and creation. It was never a pyramid.

The Wave Model

In 1962, psychologists David Krech, Richard Crutchfield, and Egerton Ballachey proposed a more flexible and fluid interpretation of Maslow's hierarchy of needs in their book *Individual in Society*.[25]

Crutchfield, a pioneer in group dynamics, and Ballachey, an expert in applied human behavior, argued that human motivation does not unfold in fixed steps but in overlapping patterns. On page 77, they presented what they described as "a schematic portrayal of the progressive changes in relative saliency, number, and variety of wants as described by Maslow." Their model—now known as the *Wave Model of Needs*—depicts each need, from safety to belonging to esteem, as a curve that rises and falls in intensity over time.

Unlike the rigid pyramid, where one level must be fully satisfied before the next begins to emerge, the *Wave Model* shows that higher needs awaken even as lower ones remain active.

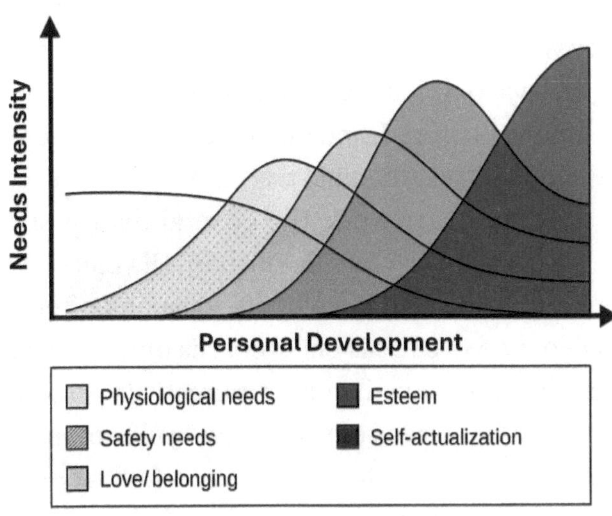

Figure 2.1 Dynamic hierarchy of needs of Abraham Maslow.[26]

As hunger fades, the desire for safety strengthens. As safety strengthens, the need for belonging, recognition, and purpose grows more distinct. And even in deprivation, those higher needs do not disappear—they simply quiet beneath the louder demands of survival.

It is a more realistic view of human life.

Needs are not boxes to be checked or levels to be cleared, but forces that coexist, each expanding or receding according to circumstance. A hungry person still longs for love. An insecure employee still dreams of achievement. The wave model reflects what experience confirms: our inner drives are overlapping, not sequential.

In simple words, we may pursue esteem and self-actualization even if we do not have love or safety.

A striking example of this interplay is found in Albert Einstein. In 1914, after years of emotional distance, Einstein separated from his wife, Mileva Marić. It was one of the most difficult years of his life—lonely, fractured, and filled with personal tension. And yet, between 1914 and 1915, amid that turmoil, Einstein completed his most revolutionary work: the general theory of relativity. As Walter Isaacson recounts in *Einstein: His Life and Universe* (2007),[27] Einstein was consumed by his equations, often forgetting to eat, sleep, or write to his children. His unmet needs for love and belonging did not extinguish his creativity; they seemed to amplify the higher waves of esteem and self-actualization. He was a man simultaneously deprived and fulfilled—hungry for connection yet completely absorbed in meaning.

Einstein's story reveals what the wave model makes visible: that human needs are not fixed rungs on a ladder but currents in motion. We do not climb them—we are carried by them. Even when fractured, the human spirit can rise, propelled by the rhythm of its deepest needs—the longing to matter, to understand, and to create. The basic needs never vanish. They remain as foundations, shaping how the higher ones move. When hunger, fear, or exhaustion grow overwhelming, the upper waves lose amplitude. Motivation weakens when the base is unstable.

But when those basic needs are met—even partially—the higher needs surge upward with remarkable power.

The Intensity of Needs

Maslow noticed that needs do not affect everyone with the same force. For one person, security drives every decision; for another, the desire to create is much more important than comfort. Everyone has their own unique mix of motivations.[28]

However, there is a common pattern. Once our basic needs for safety and belonging are mostly met, our higher needs begin to take over with even greater strength. The drive for esteem and self-actualization does not go away when it is fulfilled; it actually grows. Maslow called this "growth motivation." [29]. Basic needs motivate us to fix a problem (like hunger), so they stop driving us once we are satisfied. Higher needs motivate us to reach our potential, so they keep pushing us forward.

This dynamic is clearly shown in the Wave Model of Needs. If you look at the overlapping waves, the peaks get taller as they move toward personal development. This illustrates a key psychological truth: our higher needs actually reach a stronger intensity than our basic survival needs.

Suppressed Needs — The Hidden Needs

As sales professionals, we are experts at uncovering needs. We know how to ask open-ended questions that invite dialogue, and how to share observations that draw a deeper response. It's second nature to seek feedback—to test whether our solution truly aligns with what matters to them. Identifying technical goals and pain points is a foundational skill. After all, most customers agree to meet because they have a problem to solve or a target to hit.

But as we know, solving the technical issue alone rarely wins the deal. In fact, it's often the moment we present the solution that doubts begin to surface. The customer hesitates. Questions arise. These reactions are commonly labelled as roadblocks or objections.

Many sales trainers teach us to welcome objections. They argue that objections aren't the end of the road but signs of engagement—proof the customer is still thinking. And they're right. A disengaged customer goes silent; an interested one raises concerns because they want to move forward. They just need help crossing the gap. Skillfully addressing objections isn't a detour—it's often the very path that leads to the close.

You already know the common objections in your field. You've faced them, built slides for them, refined your answers. Since every product and sales cycle is unique, it wouldn't make sense to offer generic objection-handling tactics in a book about psychology. Our goal here is different. We aim to uncover the need behind the objection—the deeper concern that fuels resistance—and show how to address it.

We define these as *Suppressed Needs*. They remain hidden for one of two reasons: either the customer is actively protecting them, or the customer is not yet fully aware of them. Every technical or business objection can be traced back to a fundamental human need—one that fits somewhere within Maslow's hierarchy. Of course, when a customer says, "The price is too high," we must address it practically—through discounts, payment terms, or added value.

That's part of doing business. But in most cases, something deeper is also at play—a psychological driver, a hidden need.

Take the familiar pricing objection.

The same words—"It's too expensive"—can arise from entirely different motives. When I hear this from a purchasing manager, it's often not just about the budget. It may be about esteem: achieving discount goals, earning praise, or proving negotiation skills. But when the same objection comes from a VP of R&D, the story changes. Sometimes it is a need for safety: he is over budget, under pressure, and trying to protect his team. Other times, it is a need for belonging: a desire to align with upper management by aggressively challenging a supplier's price. The reality is that people rarely reveal their personal motives. A customer may speak of "budget constraints," but they won't mention that earning a better price could win them praise from the CEO. They'll talk about timelines or specs—but not about fear, pride, or pressure.

**The heart is deceitful above all things and beyond cure.
Who can understand it?**

— Jeremiah 17:9

We all mask our insecurities and soften our desires. No one would walk into a meeting and say, "I want to feel respected," or "I need to prove myself." Revealing true motives takes trust—and sometimes even self-awareness we don't yet have. Salespeople build relationships precisely to reach this depth of understanding. It's in open, genuine conversations—over coffee, or after a meeting—where we start to hear what truly matters: not the specs or deadlines, but the personal stakes, the hidden pressures, the unspoken goals. Every salesperson knows the moment when understanding clicks—when you finally see what's really driving the customer. That knowledge is the most valuable asset in any negotiation.

The salesperson who grabs the full picture can outshine the competition. Once you know what the other side must protect—and what they hope to achieve—you can work with their energy instead of against it. But without that knowledge, you're blind and deaf.

A true story: A colleague of mine pitched a technically flawless solution to the VP of Engineering at a major tech company. On paper, it was perfect: faster, cheaper, better. We walked out certain we had the deal. Then—nothing. No call, no follow-up. A week later, a polite request for small changes. Then silence again. Eventually, we learned the deal went to a competitor offering a slightly weaker solution. It didn't make sense—until someone who knew the VP personally told us why. He'd recently been passed over for a promotion and was under pressure to prove his strategic worth. He didn't just need a product; he needed a win. He wanted to walk into that boardroom and say, "Here's how I saved us money and future-proofed our platform." He wanted recognition. We offered the better system—but the competitor offered the better story. They met his esteem need. We missed the motive—and lost the deal.

Every salesperson knows that relationships create trust, and trust opens doors. But even strong relationships don't guarantee full access to someone's inner world. Just as we don't share everything with friends or family, customers don't share everything with us. And here's the truth: most people aren't even fully honest with themselves. If they were, psychologists would be out of work. Think about it.

How often do we truly understand what's bothering us in the moment? That sting of jealousy, that discomfort, that defensiveness—what's behind it? Is it fear, esteem, belonging, or safety?

We can't always tell. If it's this hard to understand ourselves, imagine how hard it is to read a customer in a one-hour meeting. That's why uncovering true motivation isn't just about asking questions—it's about learning to listen between the lines. It requires recognizing that we cannot infer a person's needs simply based on their job title.

So, why bother understanding them? Why analyze customers psychologically when our solution is already strong? Because that is the job. Technical teams can perfect the specs. Finance can shape the deal. But the salesperson's true work is to uncover the real drivers behind every decision—to see what others overlook. In complex sales, that means understanding the suppressed needs of every stakeholder, not just what they say but what they conceal.

Suppressed Customer Needs

Experienced sales professionals build intuition through thousands of face-to-face interactions. Their interpersonal skills feel automatic, but they are actually the result of years of trial and error. You cannot simply memorize how to identify suppressed needs and hidden motives; you must practice finding them in the real world. Emotional intelligence is an active skill, not just a set of facts.

> **To develop knowledge, we must learn. To develop skill, we must practice.**
>
> *— Ariel Feder*

This chapter provides a practical framework for spotting those hidden motives. Think of it as your starting point. The more you exercise these concepts in actual meetings, the sharper your instincts will become.

It always starts with a feeling: listening to your gut. We have all experienced that nagging sense that something is slightly "off" during a customer interaction. Maybe the meeting feels suspiciously easy, or perhaps the customer is reacting irrationally to a minor detail. That lingering unease is your intuition telling you to look deeper. By testing that gut feeling against the framework in this chapter, you can uncover the real truth—and act on it.

Yet many of us overlook that feeling.

We brush aside our intuition, trusting the customer's words more than our own perception. It often happens not out of denial but convenience—we prefer to deal with what's visible and measurable. Addressing only the stated issue feels efficient and safe. But when we ignore what lies beneath, the unspoken concerns remain unresolved, quietly shaping the decision that follows. This is wishful thinking.

It pulls us farther from the truth, a blind spot that is deeply detrimental to both sales and negotiation. We must be courageous in seeking the truth—without hope and without fear. Truth is what matters most. Seek the truth, and you shall find it.

> *If you look for truth, you may find comfort in the end.*
> *If you look for comfort, you will not get either comfort*
> *or truth—only soft soap and wishful thinking to begin,*
> *and in the end, despair.*[30]

— *Clive Staples Lewis*

The Suppressed Needs Discovery Framework

The Suppressed Needs Discovery Framework consists of two complementary fields:

Field A: Cognitive Indicators

This field focuses on patterns of thought and decision-making—signs recognized by observing illogical or inconsistent customer behavior from a distance.

It's about stepping back, seeing the bigger picture, and noticing when something simply doesn't add up. When behavior doesn't make sense, it doesn't mean the customer is foolish. In most cases, C-level managers are smart and very professional. The illogical behavior reveals a hidden motive. Once that motive is uncovered, the behavior becomes logical—and actionable.

> *Don't judge a man until you've walked a mile in his*
> *shoes.*

— *Traditional proverb*

Field B: Behavioral Indicators

This field focuses on what can be observed in real time—the cues revealed during direct interaction with the customer. For people with developed emotional intelligence, these appear as subtle inconsistencies: a mismatch between what the customer says and how they say it—their tone, posture, gestures, or facial expressions. Such inconsistencies often signal suppressed emotions or fears.

And when emotions are suppressed, there is usually a hidden emotional need beneath the surface. By recognizing these cues and addressing them with empathy, we can help the customer process them—and gain the clarity needed to move forward with confidence.

> **When the tone of voice and body language don't match the words, the words are the lie.**[31]
>
> — *Chris Voss*

Now that we've introduced the two observation fields—Cognitive and Behavioral—let's examine each in detail. In the following pages, we'll explore the most common indicators of suppressed needs and, more importantly, how to effectively address them. These patterns aren't theoretical; they come from real-world experience, drawn from the kinds of meetings and negotiations you already know well. Once you learn to recognize these subtle signs, you'll begin to see suppressed needs everywhere—and you will finally know exactly how to act on them.

Field A: Cognitive Indicators

I. Irrationality:

When a customer's words and actions clash, it's not chaos—it's emotional leakage. Four patterns reveal suppressed needs.

Contradictions: The Internal Struggle

Imagine you're discussing a complex technology solution with a senior executive. Early in your conversation, they emphasize: "We need an innovative leap forward—something genuinely groundbreaking." Yet moments later, they caution: "But we can't afford to make any mistakes; our board is extremely risk-averse." At face value, these statements oppose each other. But rather than confusion or indecision, such contradictions usually point to internal emotional friction—fear clashing against ambition.

Suppressed Needs: Safety (*fear of failure*), Esteem (*fear of judgment*). Contradictions emerge when customers feel intense internal pressure. They deeply desire progress yet are simultaneously afraid of the repercussions of failure.

What you might say: Don't challenge contradictions directly; that triggers defensiveness. Instead, gently surface the internal tension to facilitate clarity: *"I understand you want bold innovation while managing risk carefully. Can you walk me through how you're balancing these two priorities internally right now?"*

This approach invites honest dialogue, helping customers openly acknowledge the underlying conflicts shaping their decisions.

Downplaying to Hide Failure

Have you encountered a customer who dismisses valid concerns almost instantly, claiming absolute certainty? Consider a VP of Operations confidently stating: "The failure in production isn't a big concern—we've solved these many times before." Or: "It's not important to be first to market—we'll win anyway because our solution is the best." While confidence can be reassuring, excessive bravado often signals an underlying vulnerability—a tension they're not ready to reveal. Seasoned professionals rarely brush off legitimate risks without a reason.

Suppressed Needs: Safety and Esteem. Overconfidence to shield their failures. Beneath the surface, they are anxious about failure, or about being seen as less capable than their role demands.

What you might say: Acknowledge their experience to ease ego defenses, then gently guide them towards risk awareness: "Given your extensive experience, your confidence makes sense. At the same time, experienced leaders often keep contingency plans ready. Should we briefly explore those scenarios together?" This helps lower defenses, opening a more balanced and realistic conversation about risk and responsibility.

Projection: Externalizing Hidden Doubts

You've probably witnessed clients attribute project failures or delays primarily to external factors—vendors, market volatility, or partners. They emphasize factors outside their control repeatedly. Statements like: "*It wasn't us; our previous vendor couldn't deliver,*" or "*The market shifted unpredictably,*" often contain grains of truth. But when external attribution is exaggerated, it reveals deeper insecurities.

Suppressed Need: *Esteem, Safety.* By projecting blame outward, individuals protect their self-esteem and avoid admitting personal or organizational inadequacies. It safeguards their ego and shields them from internal critique or judgment.

What you might say: Avoid direct challenge. Instead, invite shared ownership constructively: *"Those external issues sound very challenging. From your perspective, is there anything we could proactively do together to strengthen your position or mitigate future external factors?"* Positioning responsibility as collaborative rather than personal helps the client safely confront underlying concerns without damaging their self-image.

Obsession with Details: The Illusion of Control

We've all encountered customers who fixate on minutiae—whether it's obscure contractual clauses, edge-case technical specifications, or hypothetical failure scenarios. These seemingly trivial concerns often hijack strategic conversations: "Can you confirm again the exact specifications for each minor component?" While diligence is healthy, compulsive attention to detail often reveals something deeper.

Suppressed Need: Safety. The customer is trying to calm internal anxiety by focusing on something small. Something that they can control.

What you might say: "Those details are clearly important—let's document them carefully. Just to make sure we're prioritizing the right areas, can you walk me through how these specifics connect to your bigger strategic goals?" This approach acknowledges the customer's need for control, while gently guiding the conversation back to high-level alignment and value.

II. Inconsistency

In B2B sales, inconsistency is rarely random. A sudden reversal, shifting priority, or new approval layer usually signals unseen forces—internal politics, competitive pressure, or changing market dynamics. Often, it means the decision has moved upward to higher-ranking leaders such as the COO, CTO, or CEO.

> *The quicker you let go of old cheese; the sooner you find new cheese.*[32]
>
> — *Spencer Johnson*

This is the time to elevate the conversation. You need to be in the room where decisions are made. Use your own managers to open those doors—arrange a meeting between your Product Line Manager and their CTO to discuss roadmaps or introduce your VP of Sales to their COO to align strategy and priorities.

Once power shifts, inconsistency begins to show itself in different ways: through sudden decision reversals, changing goals, or role shifting driven by internal politics. Recognizing which one you're facing is the first step to responding wisely.

Decision Reversals: Management Pressure

When a confident "We've decided to move forward" suddenly becomes "Actually, we need to reconsider," something has shifted behind the scenes. Often, it means a senior stakeholder—previously silent or unseen—has stepped in late with strong opinions or a prior relationship with your competitor.

Suppressed Needs: Belonging and Esteem. Your contact fears losing alignment with influential stakeholders and protects their reputation by following powerful colleagues, even against their own judgment.

What You Might Say: Avoid direct confrontation. Instead, gently uncover the hidden influences by asking: *"It sounds like your priorities have shifted. Is there new information we should consider so we can realign our approach?"* This empathetic framing invites transparency, lowering their defenses to reveal a competitor's influence without making the customer feel interrogated.

Changing Goals Caused by Market Pressures

When "We prioritize innovation" suddenly turns into "Actually, compliance and cost-efficiency are our top priorities," something has changed. These sudden shifts are often triggered by external forces—market turbulence, investor pressure, or a rival's strong pitch to senior leadership.

Suppressed Needs: Belonging—to be part of the shift; Esteem—to maintain credibility with all parties, including you.

What You Might Say: Show awareness of external influences while inviting open disclosure: *"I've noticed the goals shifting. Has something changed internally—or perhaps in your market or investor expectations—that we should factor into our planning?"*

Role Shifting Caused by Internal Politics

Sometimes a deal that seemed approved is suddenly pulled back because a higher-ranking leader wants to reassert authority or influence. It's a quiet power struggle—an internal turf war disguised as process.

Suppressed Needs: Esteem and belonging. The customer fears losing credibility or status if they're seen promoting a decision that no longer aligns with upper management.

What You Might Say: Position yourself as an ally who reinforces their internal credibility: "Looping in senior leadership makes sense. I'd be glad to join—framed as supporting your recommendation and offering strategic insight. It strengthens your position and shows you're driving alignment."

III. Apathy

Emotions are essential in sales because emotion creates motion. If a customer isn't emotionally engaged, it means no real need is being addressed. Without emotional investment, there is no momentum. No drive. No decision.

Apathy may appear as agreement and a lack of objections—but it's a loud signal that the customer is not serious about buying. Sometimes, this shows up as a subtle shift in the conversation. You mention something meaningful—budget, timeline, risk— and the customer quickly changes the subject. It feels like a harmless detour, but it's often a clear signal. When customers divert attention away from core issues, they're not interested.

Sometimes, the warning sign is quick agreement with absolutely zero depth. You share a key proposal or insight, and they merely nod along with a hollow "Sure," or "Sounds good." Customers use this to politely block deeper engagement. It is the boardroom equivalent of asking your teenager, "How was school?" and getting the automated response: "Fine."

No emotional involvement means no need.

When you sense this kind of detachment, the most powerful move is to name it—calmly, professionally, and without judgment. You might say: "To *deliver meaningful value, we need to understand what you need. If it is not clear yet, perhaps we should meet another time.*"

Field B: Behavioral Indicators

Customer behavior in meetings often reveals more about their suppressed needs and motives than they intend to share. A subtle misalignment between their words and voice—or between their statements and body language—can speak louder than any objection.

I. Vocal

You've probably heard it in meetings—the customer says all the right words, but something in their voice feels... off. The pitch doesn't quite match the confidence. They laugh when nothing is funny. They agree, but in a tone so flat it sounds more like a dare than alignment.

These aren't just gut feelings. They're consistent patterns—recognized in behavioral psychology research and confirmed by AI analysis across tens of thousands of sales conversations. These are vocal leaks: moments when the mouth says "yes," but the nervous system quietly says, "not really." When you hear them, you're no longer dealing with logic alone. You're witnessing suppressed needs—often safety, esteem, or belonging. Let's break down the three clearest vocal cues:

Elevated Pitch

One of the easiest signs to miss—and one of the most revealing—is when a customer ends a confident-sounding sentence with a question mark instead of a period. "We're pretty confident in that?" It's subtle, but the tone rises instead of falling. The words try to land with certainty, but the voice lifts off at the end—like it's looking for permission or quietly second-guessing itself. This isn't just habit. It's a known behavioral pattern. Linguistic research has long linked rising pitch at the end of a declarative sentence—known as a *rising declarative*—to uncertainty or lack of commitment [33]. More recently, AI tools analyzing thousands of sales conversations have identified the same signal: "Rising intonation might signal a question or uncertainty. Models trained on diverse tonal patterns can infer customer satisfaction or frustration even if the words themselves are neutral".[34]

What you're hearing is a clash between language and emotion—often tied to suppressed needs like esteem or safety. They may be unsure of their stance, afraid to be wrong, or bracing for pushback.

Once you spot this, it is a good time to explore what might be beneath the surface—just don't push too hard. Shift the topic, build trust, and come back to it when the moment feels right.

Nervous Laughter

Sometimes, it's not the words but the soft chuckle that gives them away—especially when there's nothing funny happening. Picture this: you ask, "Would the CTO be aligned on this?" and they reply, "Heh... yeah... probably?" That laugh isn't humor—it's a pressure release. Psychologists call it coping laughter, an involuntary response when emotional tension spikes under stress or social discomfort.

This is a classic sign of a suppressed safety need—fear of saying the wrong thing, internal politics, or the risk of being scrutinized. Academic research shows that nervous laughter often appears in moments of status threat or emotional tension.[35] AI has enabled sales tools like Gong and Chorus.ai to detect such laughter in real-time, flagging it as erratic vocal energy signaling hesitation or undeclared conflict.[36] [37]

What you're hearing is emotional friction. It is time to take notes, step back, and earn the trust that will let the real conversation surface later.

The Flat or Sarcastic Tone

When a customer says something like "That's great," but the tone is flat and robotic—or worse, blandly sarcastic ("Oh yeah, amazing")—you're not hearing real agreement. You're hearing emotional distance. It often means they disagree, or simply don't care, but don't feel safe enough to say so directly. Instead, they tuck the objection inside polite words. This pattern often reflects suppressed needs for esteem or belonging—the fear of sounding combative, or the feeling that their input doesn't matter. As Keltner and Bonanno observed, emotional signals like tone often leak in subtle ways when people mask discomfort in social situations.[38]

AI systems trained on acoustic sentiment have picked up the same signals. Flat or sarcastic tones in customer conversations are consistently associated with emotional disengagement and low purchase intent (WayWithWords).[39]

II. Timing

The timing of responses, hesitation before key points, and the frequency with which customers revisit certain topics can speak volumes about their hidden emotional needs. These subtle but powerful signals reveal underlying emotional tension, internal doubts, or suppressed objections that customers aren't ready or able to openly express.

Delayed Response

I once asked a VP of Product if the new scope aligned with her CEO's priorities. She smiled, opened her mouth—and paused. Two seconds. Then came a careful, "It should be fine." That moment stuck with me. The pause wasn't confusion—it was caution. Later, she admitted her CEO hadn't seen the deck at all.

In sales conversations, these small silences say a lot. Based on Stockholm University research, people respond within 300 to 800 milliseconds.[40] When that timing breaks—especially before a key decision—it's often emotional, not logical.

AI tools like Gong and Uniphore now flag these pauses in real time, linking them to uncertainty, internal misalignment, or suppressed objections.[41]

And recent linguistic research backs this up: characteristic delays usually indicate internal friction or cognitive load, not thoughtful reflection.[42]

In those cases, it's critical not to fill the uncomfortable silence. Doing so may prevent you from hearing the customer's true answer to a difficult question. In general, your team should be trained never to answer questions that were directed at the customer.

Frequency of a Topic

When a customer revisits the same topic again and again, it's rarely accidental. In one deal, a procurement lead brought up integration risks five separate times across three meetings. On the surface, it sounded like repetition. In reality, it was fixation. Repeatedly circling back to one issue is often a sign that it holds emotional weight—something unresolved, uncertain, or politically sensitive. It's like a mental loop: the customer's mind drifts back to the topic because it represents their core concern.

Behavioral research and AI analysis agree—topic recurrence is a reliable indicator of underlying tension.[43] [44] We see this behavior in daily life. Think of a child waiting for ice cream: you have already promised it, but until it is in their hand, they cannot think or talk about anything else. Adults do the exact same thing when it comes to unresolved fears in high-stakes decisions. It is smart to proactively loop back to the emotional subject. This shows that you recognize its importance, and that you're here to help resolve it. Until that core concern is addressed, they won't be able to focus on anything else—and they certainly won't move forward.

III. Body Language

We all know the basics of body language, like crossed arms or nervous fidgeting. But CEOs and VPs seldom act as explicitly as children. In high-stakes B2B conversations, the real signals are subtle.

The soul is a spider, the body its web.[45]

— Heraclitus

Lip Compression and Face-Touching

Imagine this: you're explaining value, and the customer nods politely. But then their lips press into a tight line, or their hand grazes their chin, nose, or mouth. What would you feel? In my experience, those subtle expressions are the most common in meeting rooms. Other body language signals might be too obvious—so they're socially acceptable, even ignored. But these small gestures are different. They are quiet indicators that something deeper is happening beneath the surface. These findings are spotted by computer vision systems as patterns in millions of video frames[46] [47] [48] and grounded in decades of behavioral psychology research. Lip compression and face-touching are reliable signals of internal conflict.

Lip compression is a classic self-regulation cue, often appearing when someone wants to speak up but holds back. It marks a moment of internal disagreement or emotional suppression—tension around price, fear of exposure, or friction they can't yet voice. As former FBI agent Joe Navarro explains, it's the body saying, *"I feel something—but I can't let it out."*[49]

Face-touching, particularly around the mouth or jaw, is another subtle but powerful tell. Research by DePaulo et al.[50] shows it increases under stress, especially when someone is withholding or managing discomfort. These movements act as subconscious self-soothing—a sign the person feels unsafe, uncertain, or emotionally exposed. Ekman and Friesen[51] defined these gestures as part of the *nonverbal leakage system*—brief, unconscious expressions of suppressed emotional states. When both lip compression and face-touching appear together, they often signal what Vrij and Granhag[52] call *cognitive strain*: the moment a person is navigating internal conflict, weighing risk, or preparing to withhold true intent.

In those moments, your best move isn't to push for a close—it's to pause. Reflect, clarify, or soften the pressure. These gestures aren't rejection; they're visible signs of an invisible need—usually tied to safety, belonging, or esteem.

Lack of Mirroring

You lean in slightly. You soften your tone. You offer a friendly smile. But across the table—nothing. No smile in return. No mirrored posture. Just stillness.

At first, it's easy to overlook. After all, the words might still sound agreeable. But in human connection, absence is often louder than presence.

Psychologists call this the *chameleon effect*—an automatic, unconscious tendency to mimic the body language, tone, and gestures of those we feel aligned with.[53] When people feel connected, they mirror. When they don't, they don't. Later studies confirmed this: mimicry is a social glue, a signal of trust and emotional alignment.[54]

AI systems like Sybill track this in real time, as one of the predictors of deal loss. When mirroring disappears, it's a red flag—often a sign that something you said disrupted the emotional balance. When you notice it, pause. Rewarm the space with lightness, humor, or genuine curiosity—something that reopens connection. At the same time, pay attention. What was the trigger? What changed? If *you* became the reason they withdrew, the deal won't recover until the trust does.[55]

Architecting the Final Decision: The Deal Plan and the Value Proposition

Now that we can spot both stated and suppressed needs, we must translate them into a value proposition that speaks to the deepest drivers behind a decision.

In complex B2B sales, a winning value proposition is never built for your champion alone. With buying groups typically spanning six to ten stakeholders—each bringing competing priorities and hidden fears to the table—the salesperson must shift from pitching to orchestrating. The goal is to align your solution with the emotional and practical needs of every individual, unifying a divided room around a shared vision of success.

The data proves why this is vital. Gartner research shows that B2B buyers spend only 17% of their journey meeting with suppliers, leaving you with perhaps 5% of their total time.[56] The rest is spent internally, fighting through a messy, nonlinear consensus process. As Matthew Dixon and Brent Adamson famously highlighted in their groundbreaking book, *The Challenger Sale*, this exact internal complexity overwhelms customers and frequently ends in the ultimate deal-killer: "no decision" paralysis.[57]

The only way to prevent this paralysis is to guide the buying group through their own internal alignment.[58] We orchestrate this alignment to prepare for one specific event: the final decision-making meeting.

This is the most critical moment of the sales cycle. Months of relationship-building, product demos, and negotiations all come down to a single room—and you will not be invited. This is why we relentlessly uncover suppressed needs beforehand. By addressing every stakeholder's hidden motives early on, we ensure no last-minute objections resurface when we aren't there to defend the deal. When the buying group finally sits down to choose, our orchestration ensures the choice is already made.

The Deal Plan

To win the final decision, you must act long before the final internal meeting takes place. You need a strategic blueprint that tailors your Value Proposition to the exact psychological profile of every person in the buying group. This is where the *Deal Plan* comes in.

A *Deal Plan* is a table mapping major stakeholders, roles, expressed and suppressed needs, and our message.

Stakeholder	Role	Expressed Needs	Suppressed Needs	Our Message	The Messenger	Timing
Product Owner	Day-to-day sponsor	Usability, delivery speed	Anxiety over team workload (Safety)	Fast deployment, minimal disruption, trainings	Solution Consultant	First
COO	Strategic decision-maker	Efficiency, innovation, scalability	Fear of failure (Esteem), Internal politics (Belonging)	Strategic alignment, risk mitigation	Product Manager	Early-mid stage
R&D Director	Technical authority	Performance, integration	Lack of influence (Esteem), Overwhelm (Safety)	Technical edge, engineering support, roadmap	Application Engineer	Early stage
Procurement Manager	Commercial gatekeeper	Cost control, compliance	Lack of trust (Safety), Rigidity (Esteem)	TCO, contractual flexibility, vendor reliability	Account Executive	Mid-late stage
CFO	Budget authority	ROI, cost transparency	Loss of control (Esteem), Sunk cost (Safety)	Financial justification, cost of inaction	Sales Director	Late stage

Table 2.1 — Example of a Deal Plan table.

Let us break down the Deal Plan, column by column, to orchestrate a winning consensus:

5. Stakeholder & Role

This defines who the key decision-makers are. In most cases, it would be the Product Owner (the day-to-day sponsor), Procurement Manager (the commercial gatekeeper), CEO of the company, and others.

6. Expressed Needs

These are the business requirements the stakeholder states out loud.

Example: The COO explicitly asks for "efficiency, innovation, and scalability." The CFO asks for "ROI and cost reduction."

7. Suppressed Needs

This is the core of your strategy. What is the stakeholder *really* worried about but won't say out loud? Using the Suppressed Needs Discovery framework, you identify the hidden forces shaping their choices.

Example: The R&D Director might express a need for "performance and integration." But beneath the surface, they may feel overwhelmed by their current workload (Safety) and fear that an outside solution will diminish their internal influence (Esteem).

8. Our Message

Once you know both the Expressed and Suppressed needs, you can craft a targeted message. You do not just pitch the product's features; you frame the solution to resolve their suppressed needs.

Example: To win over that R&D Director, you don't just give a standard software demo. You focus the message on providing a "technical edge and engineering support." This reassures them that they aren't losing control, but rather gaining a powerful tool that makes them look like a visionary leader.

9. Messenger

The best message will fail if delivered by the wrong person. Great sales professionals act as orchestrators, deploying the most suitable colleague to build trust with specific stakeholders. People trust their peers.

Example: Send an Application Engineer to speak with the R&D Director. Send a Regional Sales Manager to speak with the CFO. When stakeholders speak with someone who "speaks their language," their defensive barriers (Safety needs) naturally lower.

10. Timing

Not all stakeholders should be engaged at once. The Deal Plan dictates the sequence of your outreach to build momentum. Some stakeholders should be approached only after you speak with their peers.

Example: You engage the Product Owner *first* to secure an internal champion. You bring in the CFO in the *late stages* once the technical and strategic value has already been proven, making the financial justification much easier to swallow.

Crafting the Value Proposition for the Deal Plan

As you can see from the "Our Message" column, your Value Proposition is not just a slide deck—it's your narrative!

A Value Proposition should address all levels of the customer's motivational structure. It speaks to basic needs like cost, timelines, and risk (Safety), while also addressing higher-order needs like esteem and self-actualization. It frames your offer in terms of what each stakeholder truly values.

While the baseline value proposition to an account contains products, services, support, and a price, the word "Value" ultimately addresses the value *to the customer*. In other words, how this deal will help the stakeholder fulfill their unique expressed and suppressed needs.

Because the needs of every stakeholder are different, it is only logical that we must adjust the Value Proposition for each individual. To properly fill out your Deal Plan and build these tailored narratives, your team should ask the following six questions:

- What are the stakeholder's expressed and suppressed needs?

- How does our proposed deal help the stakeholder fulfill those needs?

- How can we emphasize this message in the value proposition as we present it to this stakeholder?

- Who is most suitable to convey this message to them?

- What will the stakeholder remember and tell other stakeholders?

- How does it fit into the entire organizational picture?

Based on the answers to those questions, you can emphasize the specific benefits that our deal will provide. You then adjust your value proposition presentation and arm the messenger with an effective narrative. This gives you the best chance to win over each stakeholder one by one.

We must remember: the sale isn't won by a demo. It is won in the stories your advocates tell when you are not in the room. Design those stories—or someone else will.

These tools do more than manage a deal—they shape the psychology of the decision. They move each stakeholder up the wave of needs, toward unshakeable confidence in our solution. When the internal meeting finally comes, the outcome shall be in our favor. Not just because we had a better proposal, but because we designed the psychology of the decision.

Chapter Summary:

The goal of this section is to help you remember the chapter and provide a Cheat Sheet for your work as a sales professional.

In contrast to inspiration and persuasion, Motivation drives the fulfillment of needs and desires. The wave model of Maslow's hierarchy of needs better represents human behavior than a pyramid does. The wave model emphasizes that advanced needs exert a much stronger drive than lower needs—yet lower needs must still be addressed first. Unfulfilled basic needs will affect the customer's drive.

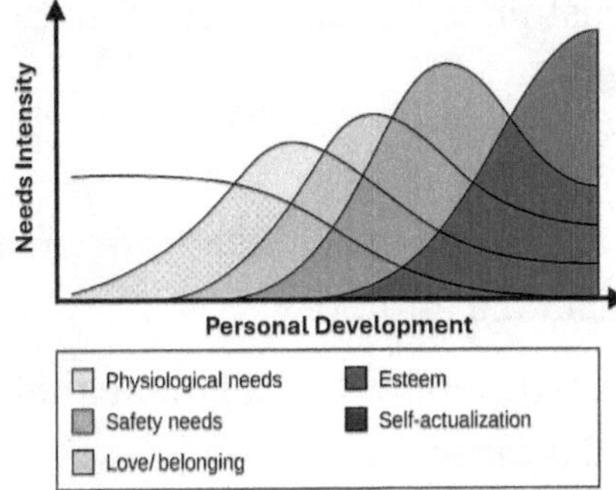

Humans do not openly share their needs with others—and in many cases, they are not fully aware of their needs themselves. Those are *Suppressed Needs*. We must discover these suppressed needs and fulfill them. Suppressed needs manifest as strange or irrational behaviors that appear illogical to us on the surface.

The Suppressed Needs Discovery Framework consists of two fields: **Cognitive** and **Behavioral.**

Here is how to uncover and identify those needs:

Field A: Cognitive Indicators

1. Irrationality

A. Contradictions

The customer expresses conflicting goals (e.g., "We want innovation" and "We must avoid risk").

Suppressed Needs: Safety, Esteem.

Fear of failure or judgment is clashing with ambition or the need to impress others.

Suggested Action: Acknowledge both drivers without forcing resolution. Invite open discussion.

B. Downplaying

The customer minimizes legitimate concerns with overconfidence.

Suppressed Need: Esteem.

They are masking self-doubt or anxiety to protect their ego and maintain authority.

Suggested Action: Compliment their experience, then guide toward awareness of risk.

C. Projection

Blames external parties (vendors, market shifts) instead of internal issues.

Suppressed Needs: Esteem, Safety.

They're protecting their self-image by externalizing blame and avoiding internal accountability.

Suggested Action: Acknowledge and redirect forward-looking conversation.

D. Obsessing Over Minor Details

Fixation on small, technical points unrelated to strategic goals.

Suppressed Need: Safety.

When overwhelmed, people zoom in on details to create the illusion of control.

Suggested Action: Help them feel control.

2. Inconsistency

A. Decision Reversals

A previous "yes" turns into hesitation or delay.

Suppressed Needs: Belonging, Esteem.

Unseen stakeholder influence.

Suggested Action: Ask about internal changes.

B. Changing Goals

Success criteria shift significantly during the process.

Suppressed Needs: Belonging, Esteem.

The board, investors, competitors are reshaping priorities.

Suggested Action: Normalize the shift, then ask about root causes.

C. Role Shifting

The ownership of the project moved to another person.

Suppressed Needs: Safety, Esteem.

Management changed priorities.

Suggested Action: Ask for senior management meeting.

3. Apathy

Emotional flatness.

Suppressed Need: No need.

There is no need for our solution. No motivation to act.

Suggested Action: Call out the lack of interest.

Field B: Behavioral Indicators

1. Vocal

A. Elevated Pitch

A confident sentence ends like a question ("We're confident in this?").

Suppressed Needs: Esteem, Safety.

Holding information for self-protection.

Suggested Action: Shift topics temporarily. Understand the hesitation.

B. Nervous Laughter

Inappropriate chuckling in moments of pressure.

Suppressed Need: Safety.

A subconscious release of anxiety.

Suggested Action: Step back from pressure. Focus on rapport-building before revisiting difficult subjects.

C. Flat or Sarcastic Tone

No emotional energy or cynicism.

Suppressed Needs: Esteem, Belonging.

Discomfort, disagreement, or disengagement masked by politeness or passive defiance.

Suggested Action: Re-engage emotionally. Use warmth or curiosity to reestablish connection.

2. Time

A. Delay in reply

Long pause before answering a key question.

Suppressed Needs: Esteem, Safety, Belonging.

Signals internal conflict. The question touches a sensitive topic, or it is a complicated subject. Suggested Action: Respect the silence. Don't rush to fill it. Listen!

B. Frequency of a Topic

Return to the same topic many times.

Suppressed Needs: Safety.

The issue carries unresolved emotional weight, usually fear, doubt, or political risk.

Suggested Action: Circle back and address it proactively.

3. Body Language

A. Lip Compression & Face-Touching

Tightly pressed lips, touching nose or mouth when challenged.

Suppressed Needs: Safety, Belonging.

Signals emotional suppression—an urge to speak or push back that's being internally restrained.

Suggested Action: Slow down. Signal safety, then revisit the issue later. Resolve the conflict.

B. Lack of Mirroring

No replication of your body language, tone, or facial expression.

Suppressed Need: Belonging.

Trust has weakened, and rapport is broken.

Suggested Action: Lighten the mood with a joke. Rebuild trust. Re-engage on a personal level.

Deal Plan and Value Proposition

Stakeholder	Role	Expressed Needs	Suppressed Needs	Our Message	The Messenger	Timing
Product Owner	Day-to-day sponsor	Usability, delivery speed	Anxiety over team workload (Safety)	Fast deployment, minimal disruption, trainings	Solution Consultant	First
COO	Strategic decision-maker	Efficiency, innovation, scalability	Fear of failure (Esteem), Internal politics (Belonging)	Strategic alignment, risk mitigation	Product Manager	Early-mid stage
R&D Director	Technical authority	Performance, integration	Lack of influence (Esteem), Overwhelm (Safety)	Technical edge, engineering support, roadmap	Application Engineer	Early stage
Procurement Manager	Commercial gatekeeper	Cost control, compliance	Lack of trust (Safety), Rigidity (Esteem)	TCO, contractual flexibility, vendor reliability	Account Executive	Mid-late stage
CFO	Budget authority	ROI, cost transparency	Loss of control (Esteem), Sunk cost (Safety)	Financial justification, cost of inaction	Sales Director	Late stage

The **Deal Plan** is a table mapping major stakeholders, their influence, expressed and suppressed needs. It states the message that we should convey to a specific stakeholder and who is most suitable to convey it.

The **Value Proposition** is a presentation or a document communicating our narrative! It is adjusted for each stakeholder to fulfill both his official and suppressed needs. In preparation of the **Value Proposition,** we should ask ourselves the following questions:

- What are the stakeholder's expressed and suppressed needs?

- How does our proposed deal help the stakeholder fulfill those needs?

- How can we emphasize this message in the value proposition as we present it to this stakeholder?

- Who is most suitable to convey this message to them?

- What will the stakeholder remember and tell other stakeholders?

- How does it fit into the entire organizational picture?

We should remember:

The sale isn't won by a demo. It's won in the stories your advocates tell when you're not in the room.

Design those stories—or someone else will.

- Ariel Feder

CHAPTER 3

Persuasion

The conference room sat on the 27th floor, its glass walls opening onto New York's skyline. The afternoon light painted the table in gold, but the mood was anything but warm.

Susan, the CIO of one of the city's largest banks, sat with her back straight, shoulders set in quiet authority. Years of boardrooms and crises had etched fine lines around her eyes—not from age, but from stress. Beside her, Karim, her deputy, tapped a pen nervously on his notepad. Younger, sharper, with dark circles under his eyes, he looked like someone who had carried too much adrenaline for too many months.

Across sat David, the cybersecurity consultant. He wasn't flashy. His suit was simple, his tablet still closed. He studied the two executives, not rushing to speak. He knew this wasn't about blasting them with slides. This was about earning trust.

Connect

David broke the silence.

"I heard about the phishing attack you dealt with last quarter," he said. "Two a.m. war rooms, customers on edge, your team firefighting."

Susan's jaw tightened. She glanced at Karim, then back at David.

"That night..." Her voice carried both control and fatigue. "That night was hell. Every system alert felt like a ticking bomb."

Karim exhaled sharply. "We kept it contained, but I'll be honest—morale hasn't recovered. My team jumps every time an email looks suspicious. We're still living in that night."

David nodded and leaned forward, his voice quieter now, almost conspiratorial.

"I know that feeling. I've sat in those same war rooms, watching dashboards light up red, praying the next alert isn't the one that takes everything down. That kind of constant pressure took a massive toll on me. Honestly, it took a long time just to feel like my normal self again."

Karim's pen stopped tapping. Susan's posture eased and she looked at David. David wasn't just a sales guy. He was one of them.

Frame

"Here is the reality," David said, straightening in his chair. "What happened to you wasn't unique."

Susan raised an eyebrow, her tone sharp. "Not unique? We thought we were targeted for a reason."

"You were," David said, "but so was almost every other bank in your sector. Seventy-eight percent faced the same type of breach last year. Most of them believed they were better prepared than average—right until the breach hit. Everyone thinks their defenses are stronger, their teams more disciplined, their processes tighter. But in reality?" David spread his hands. "What you're experiencing is standard. The defenses that once made you feel ahead are now just... table stakes."

Karim shifted in his seat. "So, what we thought was our strength... is actually just average?"

"That's exactly it," David said gently. "And when something is average, it stops being a shield. It becomes a liability. The very belief that you're unique blinds you to the gaps that are widening under your feet."

Susan's brow furrowed. She had built her career on being ahead of the curve—and now the ground beneath her advantage was giving way.

Solve

David opened his tablet, sliding it across the table so Susan and Karim could see. The screen displayed three pathways, free of jargon.

"The first option," he began, "is what you're already doing—patching the old system. It's quick, low effort, but every patch adds weight. Each layer makes the system heavier, more fragile, and easier for attackers to exploit. They only need to find one weak spot, and you're back in the war room."

He swiped to the next slide. "The second option is what many banks try: adding more tools. Another console, another stream of alerts, another layer of training. On paper, it looks stronger. In practice, it buries your team in complexity. Visibility shrinks, fatigue grows, and costs climb. It's protection by addition, but not by design."

Then David paused, letting the tension build before moving to the third slide. The layout shifted to a simple three-tiered architecture. "The third option is different. It's a unified design, three layers working together as one system. At the top, a real-time detection engine scans traffic in milliseconds, catching anomalies before they spread. Underneath, a global threat intelligence cloud pulls in data from hundreds of institutions, so your defenses learn from every attempted breach anywhere in the network, not just your own. And finally, an automated response layer isolates and neutralizes threats the moment they're detected, often before your analysts even log in—though they still see everything and remain in control."

He tapped the screen once more, freezing the diagram in front of them. "It's modular, so you can start small—with detection— then expand into intelligence and automation. Each phase is measurable, each one proven. And it's already running in over a hundred banks worldwide."

Susan leaned forward, her executive composure giving way to focus. Karim's pen began moving again—this time sketching a rough outline of what the system might look like in their own infrastructure.

"This doesn't look impossible," Karim said at last, almost under his breath.

David smiled faintly. "Exactly. Cybersecurity shouldn't feel like chaos. It should feel like control."

Vision

David leaned in, lowering his voice again.

"Picture this, six months from now. A phishing email slips through. But instead of panic, your system quarantines it instantly. The SOC team sees the alert, but pulses stay steady. They know it is handled. The attacker's tactics are fed into your global defense, strengthening your shield for the next attempt. No more two a.m. war rooms. No firefighting. Just resilience."

Karim smiled for the first time all meeting. "You make it sound... peaceful."

Susan allowed herself a dry chuckle. "Peaceful isn't usually the word we use around here."

"Exactly," David said. "And yet that's what you can lead. Not just a bank that survived an attack, but a bank your customers trust because they never even felt the attack happen."

For a moment, Susan didn't see dashboards and breach reports. She saw a board meeting where she delivered calm, confident numbers. And in that picture, she wasn't exhausted. She was respected.

Commit

David closed his tablet and sat back. No pressure in his voice, just certainty.

"Here's the next step. If you're ready, we schedule a pilot with your red team next Monday. Real attacks, in your environment, under your control. In two weeks, you'll know exactly how it performs. After that, you decide."

Susan turned to Karim. "What do you think?" she asked quietly.

Karim considered for a moment, then gave a small, measured nod. "It makes sense."

David leaned in. "We can begin the pilot on June 12. If it proves successful, the next stage would be implementing it on a small cluster of your system before any broader rollout."

Susan held Karim's gaze for a second, silently confirming the alignment. She turned back to David. "Schedule it," she said, extending her hand.

Karim followed, stepping forward with a warmer smile. He clasped David's hand firmly. "I'm looking forward to what your team can do for us."

From Story to Structure

From the outside, David's meeting with Susan and Karim looked like a routine pitch in yet another glass boardroom. Suits around a table, coffee cups cooling, slides ready on a tablet. But if you listened carefully, something else was happening. This wasn't a battle of features. This wasn't luck or charm. It was choreography.

Every word, every pause, every diagram was part of a rhythm that people respond to almost instinctively. Persuasion, when it works, feels natural—as if the decision was already waiting to be made. But it only feels natural because someone is guiding the process, step by step. That's what David was doing.

First, he Connected. He didn't start with dashboards or threat statistics. He started with people—their sleepless nights, their stress, the weight of leadership. Susan and Karim weren't just executives; they were human beings carrying scars from the last breach. David acknowledged that. He spoke to them as people first, managers second. And in that simple act, the defenses began to lower.

Then, he Framed their reality. With care, he held up a mirror and showed them what they had refused to admit: their defenses, once a source of pride, were now ordinary. What they thought was a differentiator was, in truth, just average. This wasn't accusation. It was awakening. Until they saw the gap between perception and reality, no solution—however brilliant—could take root.

Only after the frame was cracked did David Solve. But he didn't drown them in acronyms or endless slides. He offered clarity. Three options, each one simple, each one honest. He cut through complexity, showing a path that looked manageable instead of overwhelming. For the first time, Karim leaned in—not because he was impressed by buzzwords, but because he understood.

After the Solve came the Vision. David lifted them out of today's firefights and let them glimpse a tomorrow defined by resilience. He didn't promise miracles. He promised stability: a system that learned, a team that slept, a bank that projected calm instead of panic. And for a moment, Susan wasn't a tired CIO fighting endless fires. She was a leader presenting a confident future to her board.

Finally, David guided them to Commit. Not with pressure, not with a desperate ask, but with a next step so simple, so safe, it was easier to agree than to delay: a controlled pilot. Low risk, high reward. Easy to start, and easy to move to the next stage.

What looked like a conversation was, in fact, a journey. Not chance. Not charisma. A framework. A deliberate flow that mirrored how human beings move from doubt to conviction, from hesitation to action. This is the architecture of persuasion. And once you see it, you can never unsee it.

Why Persuasion Needs Structure

Persuasion works best as a sequence, not a single moment. Every stage has its role: first we build trust, then we reshape perspective, then we bring clarity, before guiding the client toward a future they can see and a decision they can own. When we keep this order in mind, the conversation feels natural and purposeful.

Sales conversations are rarely linear. Clients ask unexpected questions, introduce new stakeholders, or jump ahead to pricing before the groundwork is laid. In those moments, a framework acts like a compass. It reminds us where we are in the process and where we need to return. Instead of improvising under pressure, we can adjust with confidence, knowing the map will carry both us and the client forward.

That is the value of a framework: it helps us remember the flow, avoid skipping crucial steps, and keep the conversation moving toward a decision that feels right for the client. In five words, the journey becomes easy to hold in our minds:

Connect → Frame → Solve → Vision → Commit.

Part I: The Five Stages of Persuasion

Persuasion unfolds as a journey, and each stage has its own role in guiding the client from uncertainty to confident decision.

Stage 1: Connect

Every act of persuasion begins not with logic, but with human connection. Before a client can open their mind to new ideas, they must feel that you see them, hear them, and genuinely understand them. This is not small talk; it is the foundation of influence.

Chris Voss, the FBI negotiator, called it *tactical empathy*—the ability to demonstrate such deep listening that the other person says, "*That's right.*" In that moment, they are not agreeing with your solution. They are acknowledging that you have captured their reality. You've stepped into their shoes. And only then are they ready to walk with you.[59]

Carl Rogers, the father of humanistic psychology, argued that the deepest human need is to be understood without judgment. Empathic listening, he wrote, creates a space where defenses fall and honesty can emerge. In sales, this means resisting the urge to rush into features or pitches. It means slowing down, letting the client share their world, and reflecting it back with care. [60]

Dale Carnegie put it even more simply: people are persuaded more by your interest in them than by their interest in you. In How to Win Friends and Influence People, he reminded us that the deepest principle of human nature is the craving to be appreciated. When we show genuine curiosity about a client's struggles, goals, and frustrations, we meet that need.[61]

And beneath it all lies something primal: the need to belong to a tribe. Clients trust those they see as part of "us." When we speak their language, mirror their concerns, and reveal our shared experiences, we shrink the distance between seller and buyer. Suddenly, we are not outsiders offering advice—we are insiders, allies, part of their story.

Connection is not a warm-up. It is not a tactic to soften the client. It is the first stage of persuasion because it creates the soil in which every other stage can take root. Without it, logic feels cold, and solutions feel imposed. With it, trust grows and persuasion becomes a journey walked together.

Stage 2: Frame

The second stage of persuasion is about changing the way reality is understood. Clients rarely move forward simply because you present a solution. First, they must recognize that their current map no longer matches the territory. Until then, they will cling to familiar assumptions: "We don't really have a problem," or "Even if we do, it cannot be solved." The task is not to argue or push, but to gently shift the frame through which they see their situation.

Jean Piaget, in his study of human development, explained that growth happens when existing mental models no longer work. He called this process accommodation, the restructuring of thought to fit a new reality.[62]   In business conversations, this means creating the conditions for the client to realize that what once made sense no longer serves them.

Thomas Kuhn extended this principle to science itself. In *The Structure of Scientific Revolutions*, he argued that progress does not occur linearly, but through paradigm shifts. Scientists work within one worldview until contradictions pile up, forcing them to abandon the old framework and adopt a new one.[63] Clients often live within their own "normal science." They carry on as if the old rules still apply, until someone—the salesperson, in this case—points out the anomalies they can no longer ignore.

This is why Spencer Johnson's *Who Moved My Cheese?* became such a classic in management literature. Through a simple fable, it captured a universal truth: people resist change until they see that the "cheese"—their source of stability and success—has already moved. Once they accept that the old supply is gone, they begin to search for new paths.[64]

Framing is this moment of recognition. It is the point when a leader sees clearly that the world has shifted and that holding on to old assumptions is no longer an option. As Viktor Frankl reminded us, *when we cannot change the world, we must change ourselves.*[65]

Stage 3: Solve

Once trust is built and the client sees their world differently, the natural question follows: *What do we do about it?* This is the Solve stage. Here, the salesperson's role is to clarify, not overwhelm—to show that the problem is not endless chaos, but something that can be managed step by step.

The starting point is always discovery. You've listened, you've asked questions, and now you know not just the surface-level requirements but the real progress the client is trying to achieve. As Clayton Christensen[66] explained, people don't "buy products"—they hire solutions to do a job in their world. If you understand that job deeply, you can propose something that feels designed for them, not for "customers in general."

Strong solutions are rarely imposed from the outside. They are co-created. Every client organization has its politics, its unwritten rules, its internal champions. By working with an internal advocate—someone who has credibility inside the system—you turn *"your" plan* into *"our" plan*. And that shift is critical. When the client feels they've had a hand in shaping the path, they are far more likely to defend it, sell it internally, and drive it forward.

Equally important: a real solution is never one-dimensional. Decision-makers don't judge only on technical merit. They weigh the plan across multiple lenses at once. That's why the best proposals are holistic. They cover:

- Technical: Is it reliable, scalable, and does it fit with what we already have?

- Risk: What could go wrong, and how will it be contained?

- Financial: What will it cost today, what will it save tomorrow, and how does the math work?

- Schedule: When will value start to appear, and what milestones prove progress?

When a solution addresses all four dimensions in clear language, executives relax. They see you've thought about the world they actually live in—not just your own product.

But there is another trap to avoid: giving too many options. Barry Schwartz called it. The *paradox of choice*:[67] the more options people have, the harder it is to choose. In sales, this leads to paralysis. Instead, the best sales professionals offer two or three well-shaped alternatives. Not one (which feels like a take-it-or-leave-it), and not ten (which overwhelms). Just enough to compare and decide. Each option should be viable, distinct, and honest about the trade-offs—speed versus flexibility, lower cost versus more control.

When you do all this well, the room shifts. The client stops listening to "a pitch" and starts seeing their plan—technically credible, financially sound, risk-aware, and achievable on a believable timetable. At that moment, you are no longer a vendor trying to sell something. You are a partner helping them move forward.[68]

Stage 4: Vision

In *The Principles of Psychology*, William James argued that an idea is not just a thought; it is a blueprint for action. When you clearly visualize an outcome, your brain automatically organizes the steps to achieve it. A vision is not just wishful thinking—it is how the brain programs itself to act. Once your mind commits to the end goal, your behavior naturally follows.[69]

John Dewey took this further: decision is born from imagination. He called deliberation a "dramatic rehearsal" of possible lines of action—we run the future in our heads before we run it in the world. When the picture is vivid and credible, motivation tightens, hesitation fades, and action has somewhere definite to land.[70]

You see this everywhere people perform under pressure. Athletes walk the course in their minds—the start, the turns, the finish—so their bodies know the script before the starting gun fires. Architects live inside prototypes, imagining people navigating a space long before it exists. Strategic leaders draft the results they want to present six months from now, then work backward to make that picture a reality. That is why Vision is a critical stage in persuasion: once a client clearly sees the end state in their mind, the action naturally follows.

Stage 5: Commit

This stage turns "we should" into "we will." A decision spoken with a date, an owner, and a clear first step immediately reorganizes a customer's attention, turning intent into actual behavior.

Commitment can take many forms—booking a pilot, a handshake on the scope, or signing the final contract—but the psychological effect is the same: action follows commitment.

Always end the meeting with a commitment to the next step, even if it is small. Secure a calendar invite, assign named roles, and define the very next milestone.

> *A journey of a thousand miles begins with a single step.*[71]
>
> *-Laozi*

Part II: The 25 Heuristics of Persuasion

> *For though we call the incontinent man unjust in a way, he is not unjust absolutely; for his choice is in accord with reason, but his actions are contrary to it.*[72]
>
> *— Aristotle*

Human Irrationality

Over two thousand years ago, Aristotle named a phenomenon that still defines human behavior today: Akrasia[73] , or weakness of will. He observed that a person can understand what is right and still act against it. The problem is not a lack of knowledge; it is the conflict between reason and impulse, the persistent gap between intention and behavior. Irrationality, then, is not a rare malfunction, but a recurring and predictable feature of human nature.

Centuries later, behavioral economists would confirm this insight using a new language. For decades, classical economics assumed that people are rational agents who logically weigh their options and act in their best interest. But in reality, we often don't decide the way economists hope we do. We avoid effortful thinking, lean on intuition, and let context, emotion, and framing steer our choices.

This is where Nobel Prize winners Daniel Kahneman and Richard Thaler changed the field. They revealed that human deviations from logic aren't random—they're systematic, measurable, and deeply human. We fear losses more than we seek gains (*loss aversion*),[74] overvalue the first piece of information we hear (*anchoring*),[75] underestimate uncertainty, and prefer the comfort of the familiar (*status quo bias*).[76]

These tendencies arise from cognitive shortcuts known as heuristics. Heuristics are mental rules of thumb that people use to make decisions quickly and efficiently, especially under conditions of uncertainty, limited time, or incomplete information. While they help us move quickly in complex environments, they also make us vulnerable to predictable errors—a concept masterfully explored by Daniel Kahneman in his book, *Thinking, Fast and Slow*.[77] Just as Aristotle pointed to the failure to act on reason, modern behavioral science explains why that failure persists and how it shapes decision-making in business, leadership, and especially in sales.

As Zig Ziglar said, "*Selling is essentially a transfer of feeling.*"[78] And as Tom Hopkins put it, "*People buy emotionally and justify it with logic.*"[79] These aren't clichés—they are observations grounded in reality. Every experienced salesperson knows that logic alone rarely wins the deal. What wins are the fast judgments clients make, often before they're even aware of making them. What wins is how the message is framed, not just what it contains.

That's where *heuristics* come in. When you understand how people naturally think—how they interpret tone, assess options, evaluate risk, and respond to social signals—you stop pushing uphill. You learn to present your solution in a way that fits how the human brain prefers to process information. You don't force decisions.

This book offers a scientific approach to persuasion. We do not rely on charm or instinct. We're drawing from decades of research in behavioral economics and cognitive psychology. You'll learn how to apply those insights directly to sales conversations.

By understanding when and how specific heuristics tend to appear in a sales dialogue, you'll develop a reliable system for influencing decisions in a way that feels natural to the client. Not once. Every time.

This is what the most effective sales professionals do. They don't resist the way people make decisions. They recognize the mental patterns at play in each stage of the conversation and use that awareness to reduce friction and maintain momentum.

Mapping 25 Heuristics to the 5 Stages of Persuasion

In Sellchology, persuasion is a structured sequence. We move the client from initial hesitation to confident action by progressing through five stages:

Connect → Frame → Solve → Vision → Commit.

But even a well-planned conversation can fail if we ignore how people actually make decisions. That's why heuristics aren't just useful, but they're essential.

Let us revisit the model through a new lens. In this pass, we'll explore the heuristics—the mental shortcuts—that can be applied at each stage to influence decision-making.

By anchoring each heuristic to a specific stage of the model, you'll not only learn how and when to use it, but you'll also develop an intuitive grasp of the persuasive flow. Think of this as your behavioral toolkit, mapped directly to the rhythm of real conversations. This structure is intentional: it makes the ideas easier to remember, apply, and adapt in the moment.

In total, we'll review 25 heuristics, five for each stage. You will not use all of them in a single conversation. But even applying one or two well-chosen heuristics per stage can significantly enhance your impact. Each one acts like a lever, small in action and powerful in effect.

Let's walk through the model again. One stage at a time, yet this time through the lens of behavioral psychology.

Stage 1: Connect

Build emotional resonance and felt understanding. Every act of persuasion begins not with explanation, but with emotional alignment. Before a client can absorb a new idea or weigh a solution, they must feel that they've been seen, heard, and understood—not just intellectually, but interpersonally.

This stage is where trust is seeded—and where the mental shortcuts that shape human judgment begin to activate. These shortcuts, the heuristics, guide how people interpret others. And in the earliest moments of a conversation, they determine whether the door to influence will open... or quietly close.

Five heuristics power the Connect stage. Each one is supported by research—and becomes a practical tool in your hands once you know how to spot it, shape it, and use it ethically.

4. Halo Effect

Definition: A positive impression in one area (e.g., warmth, confidence) creates a "glow" that shapes how we perceive unrelated traits (e.g., intelligence, credibility).

Psychologists first documented the halo effect in teacher evaluations: when students rated a professor as warm, they also (incorrectly) rated them as more intelligent and organized, even when the content was identical. The mind does not build a full picture; it extrapolates from a few fast cues.

Why it matters: In sales, the opening minutes don't just set the mood. They set the frame. A calm tone, steady eye contact, or a well-placed pause can make your product sound better and your credibility feel stronger.

Example: Imagine you begin a call not by launching into an agenda, but by pausing and asking: "Can I ask what's weighing most on your mind this week?" That one moment of sincere interest frames the entire conversation, and everything you say after is filtered through the lens of care.

Remember: First impressions don't fade. They echo.

Source: Richard E. Nisbett and Timothy D. Wilson, "The Halo Effect: Evidence for Unconscious Alteration of Judgments."[80]

5. Social Proof

Definition: We look to others to decide what's normal, safe, and worth doing.

Social proof operates deep within the brain's safety system. If others like us have done something and succeeded, our resistance lowers. In sales, this is gold: the client doesn't want to be the first or only one making a leap.

Why it matters: When the client hears that peers they respect have faced a similar issue—and found a way through—they start imagining themselves doing the same.

Example: "A few months ago, I worked with a CFO in a company very similar to yours: same region, same tech stack, same cross-functional tension. They had almost the same hesitation you're describing now... but once they took the first step, the internal friction dropped faster than they expected."

Remember: No one wants to go first. Everyone wants to be second.

Source: Robert B. Cialdini, Influence: Science and Practice.[81]

6. In-Group Bias

Definition: We naturally trust people we perceive as part of our own group and subconsciously distance ourselves from outsiders.

This heuristic is rooted in evolutionary psychology: belonging meant survival. Even today, clients are quicker to open up to people who feel like "us." Shared identity stems from industry, role, background, or even a shared friend.

Why it matters: If you're perceived as an outsider, the client listens with caution. If you're perceived as an insider who "gets their world," they listen with curiosity.

Example: "When I worked in product, we had the exact same conflict you're describing. The roadmap was being driven by whoever shouted loudest. It took us a while to become more data driven and aligned."

Remember: People trust those who feel like part of their tribe.

Source: Marilynn B. Brewer, "The Psychology of Prejudice: Ingroup Love and Outgroup Hate?[82]

7. Reciprocal Self-Disclosure

Definition: When one person shares something personal, the other is more likely to do the same. This effect is deeply rooted in how we form human bonds.

Self-disclosure builds trust not through quantity (how much you say), but through quality—sharing something honest, contextually relevant, and appropriately timed. In a professional setting, you don't need to cross boundaries to "get personal." You can simply share work-related personal experiences.

Why it matters: In complex B2B sales, buyers naturally hide their true concerns behind corporate jargon. If you want a stakeholder to reveal the real internal politics or fears driving their decision, you cannot interrogate them. You must lower their defensive barriers by offering a piece of your own truth first.

Example: Instead of asking a dry discovery question like, "What are your main challenges?", you frame it with your own professional experience: "When I managed a team through a similar software migration, I honestly lost sleep over the risk of downtime. Is that something you're wrestling with here, or is the pressure coming from somewhere else?"

Remember: If you open up, they open up.

Source: Nancy L. Collins and Lynn Carol Miller, "Self-Disclosure and Liking: A Meta-Analytic Review."[83]

8. Affect Heuristic

Definition: People do not make decisions on facts alone. People make them based on how those facts feel. The affect heuristic describes how our emotional response to a person, situation, or product shapes our judgment—often before any logic is applied.

When something "feels good," the brain tags it as safe, aligned, and worth exploring. When it feels uncertain, cold, or pressured, even the best data gets filtered as a risk.

Why it matters: Your emotional tone is not decoration. It's infrastructure. It frames every argument, every number, and every next step. If the emotional climate is warm and confident, your message lands as supportive and trustworthy. If the tone feels transactional or rushed, even the right solution may come across as a threat. That's why it's not just what you say but the emotional environment you build around the conversation.

Examples: You can actively build this warm infrastructure through several intentional choices that signal you view the buyer as a human, not just an account:

- Culturally aware gifts: A thoughtful holiday gesture (for Christmas, Hanukkah, or Eid al-Fitr)—like a handwritten card, a smart notebook, or premium tea—establishes trust before the business conversation even begins.

- Authentic compliments: Noting something real about their leadership, clarity, or team culture.

- Curated environments: Hosting a lunch in a space that feels relaxed and human—somewhere with texture and light, rather than a noisy cafeteria or a beige boardroom.

- Shared laugh: A light comment or a shared laugh about industry chaos proves you are real, present, and in sync.

- Curiosity and empathy: Making space for how they are doing, not just what they are planning.

Remember: Feelings color the facts.

Source: Paul Slovic et al., "The Affect Heuristic."[84]

Summary of Stage 1: Connect

> *"People don't care how much you know until they know how much you care."*[85]
>
> — *Theodore Roosevelt*

Clients decide in seconds whether you are an ally or just another vendor. At this stage, warmth, presence, and authenticity matter more than features or arguments. The *Halo Effect* amplifies first impressions, *In-Group Bias* rewards belonging, and the *Affect Heuristic* reminds us that feelings color the facts. Connection is not a soft prelude. It is the foundation on which trust and influence are built. Without it, every pitch feels like pressure. With it, the door to persuasion opens wide.

Stage 2: Frame

Our goal is to help the clients see their situation in a new light. To change direction, people must realize their old map no longer matches the territory. In *Frame*, you don't push solutions. You help the client re-see reality. Heuristics like anchoring, contrast, and cognitive dissonance make that shift possible, turning hidden risks into visible problems and showing why change isn't optional but necessary.

> **If you will it, it is no dream**[86]
>
> — *Theodor Herzl*

The moment the frame shifts, the client stops defending the past and starts considering the future. The next stage of persuasion begins there.

9. Anchoring Bias

Definition: People rely too heavily on the first piece of information they receive, the "anchor." Everything that follows is unconsciously compared back to that initial point.

Psychologists Amos Tversky and Daniel Kahneman first demonstrated this by asking participants to spin a wheel of fortune with random numbers, then estimate the percentage of African nations in the UN. Incredibly, guesses were strongly influenced by the arbitrary number they had just spun, even though it was unrelated. The anchor set the frame.

Why it matters: In sales, the first benchmark, price, or performance measure you mention doesn't just inform the client—it shapes the lens through which they see every option that follows. If you don't set the anchor, the client will anchor themselves, often to the status quo, or to a competitor's number.

Example: Imagine opening a conversation not with your product, but with a credible industry stat: "Across your sector, top-quartile companies are delivering projects 20% faster than the median. Where do you see your team sitting today?"

That one anchor redefines the baseline. Now, the question isn't "Do we change?" It's "How do we close that 20% gap?"

Remember: Whoever sets frame sets the game.

Source: Amos Tversky and Daniel Kahneman, "Judgment under Uncertainty: Heuristics and Biases."[87]

10. Narrative Relabeling

Definition: Narrative relabeling renames a phenomenon to shift how people feel.

Behavioral economists have shown that words don't just decorate choices—they change them. In an "extreme dictator game," Capraro and Vanzo (2019) found that participants were far less likely to pick the selfish option when it was labeled "steal" rather than "take." Likewise, they were far more likely to pick the prosocial option when it was labeled "donate" or "be generous." The label alone shifted real economic behavior. Politicians know this well: "estate tax" becomes the "death tax," "immigrants" become "aliens."

Why it matters: In business, the right label can change dynamics. Call an existing system "mature," and it sounds dependable. Call it "legacy," and it suddenly feels outdated and risky.

Example: After World War II, many nations deliberately renamed their Ministries of War into Ministries of Defence. The armies did not change overnight, but the label softened their purpose from aggression to protection. The same dynamic plays out in sales: describe a competitor's product as a "niche solution" instead of a "custom solution," and you've already reframed the decision before the numbers are even discussed.

Remember: Rename the system and change the perception.

Source: Valerio Capraro and Andrea Vanzo, "The Power of Moral Words: Loaded Language Generates Framing Effects in the Extreme Dictator Game."[88]

11. False Uniqueness Effect

Definition: People often underestimate how common their abilities, practices, or challenges are, assuming their situation is more unique than it really is.

Psychologists Suls and Wan documented this bias in the 1980s: individuals tend to see their strengths, habits, or struggles as unusual, when in reality they are widely shared. The illusion of uniqueness protects self-esteem but blinds us to reality.

Why it matters: Clients often think their processes, constraints, or "special" ways of working set them apart. But if you validate that illusion without challenging it, you leave them stuck in the crowd while thinking they're leading it. Breaking false uniqueness opens the door to real differentiation.

Example: "You mentioned your analytics process is a differentiator. But our benchmarks show most of your competitors use the exact same approach. The real edge comes from what you add beyond that baseline."

Remember: Everybody thinks they're unique.

Source: Jerry Suls and Choi K. Wan, "In Search of the False-Uniqueness Phenomenon: Fear and Estimates of Social Consensus."[89]

12. Framing Effect

Definition: The way information is presented changes how it is perceived, even when the facts remain identical. People respond differently to a situation framed as a loss than one framed as a gain.

In 1981, Amos Tversky and Daniel Kahneman ran one of psychology's most famous experiments called "the Asian disease problem." They asked people to imagine a deadly outbreak expected to kill 600 people. Participants had to choose between two programs:

Program A (Gain Frame): "200 people will be saved."

Program B: "There's a 1/3 chance all 600 will be saved, and a 2/3 chance no one will be saved."

Most people picked Program A as the safe, guaranteed outcome.

But when the very same outcomes were framed in terms of deaths instead of saves:

Program A (Loss Frame): "400 people will die."

Program B: "There's a 1/3 chance no one will die, and a 2/3 chance all 600 will die."

Suddenly most people switched to Program B, the risky option.

Nothing changed except the frame. The math was identical. Yet the human mind reacted as if it were two entirely different problems. This simple twist revealed a profound truth: we don't choose based on logic alone; we choose based on how reality is presented to us.

Why it matters: In sales, framing changes the customer's perspective on the same data. Instead of "stable," reframe the data as losing money, and the customer will be open to hear our solution. Saying "Customer attrition is 8%" makes it sound like just another number. Saying "By year's end, that's an entire segment lost to competitors" makes it feel like a very big problem.

Example: Instead of saying: "Your infrastructure costs are 20% higher than average." You may say: "For every $1M you spend, $200K vanishes compared to your peers—that's a new hire or a product launch lost each year."

Remember: Avoiding loss drives action.

Source: Amos Tversky and Daniel Kahneman, "The Framing of Decisions and the Psychology of Choice."[90]

13. Story Bias (Narrative Fallacy)

Definition: People are far more likely to accept, trust, and remember information when it's wrapped in a coherent story rather than delivered as raw data.

Nassim Nicholas Taleb labeled this the narrative fallacy in The Black Swan: our brains are wired for meaning, so we simplify complexity into storylines: heroes, struggles, and outcomes. It's not accuracy we seek first; it's coherence. That's why a mediocre story beats flawless data almost every time.

Why it matters: In sales, facts alone rarely stick. Clients don't walk away reciting your benchmark charts—they replay the story you told. When clients hear a story that mirrors their own struggles and ends with a believable success, they begin to picture themselves in the same arc.

Example: If you pitch, "Our platform increases productivity by 25%," the prospect will just ask for the price. Instead, translate the data into a story: *"That 25% increase meant our last client hit their annual release target in September. Not one engineer worked a weekend, and they stopped losing their best people to burnout."* The prospect won't remember the percentage. They will remember getting their weekends back.

Remember: People remember stories, not spreadsheets.

Source: Nassim Nicholas Taleb, *The Black Swan: The Impact of the Highly Improbable*.[91]

Summary of Stage 2: Frame

A problem well stated is a problem half solved.[92]

— *Charles Kettering*

In this stage, the client changes how they see the situation. The moment they stop defending the status quo and start questioning it, the path to transformation begins.

Stage 3: Solve

This stage centers on the solution. The client has opened up (Connect) and seen their world in a new light (Frame). Now comes the moment they've been waiting for: the Solution. But in sales, having the right solution is never enough. The way you present it determines how powerfully it lands.

Clients like to believe they're weighing features, costs, and risks with perfect rationality. Yet decisions don't live on spreadsheets— they live in the mind. Trust flows toward authority. Risks feel heavier than opportunities. Too many options stall momentum. And when clients feel they've had a hand in shaping the answer, their ownership makes the solution irresistible.

This is where heuristics become your edge. They allow you to position your solution, so it doesn't just make sense—it feels like the natural choice.

1. Authority Bias

Definition: We tend to place greater trust in the opinions of perceived experts or authority figures, even when their expertise is only loosely related to the decision at hand.

Psychologists first demonstrated this with Milgram's obedience studies, where people followed instructions from someone in a lab coat simply because they looked authoritative.[93] In business, the same shortcut applies: when an expert speaks, clients are primed to listen.

Why it matters: Clients may review your slides and run their numbers, but what often tips the scale is who delivers the message. A technical lead, an outside expert, or even a respected client reference adds weight that data alone cannot. Authority quiets doubt and build confidence.

Example: Instead of walking through every detail yourself, you bring in your expert: "Here's Eli—he's led over a dozen rollouts just like this in the past two years. He'll walk you through the exact process and lessons learned." In that moment, the solution feels safer, clearer, and more inevitable.

Remember: When authority speaks, people listen.

Source: Charlie Munger, "The Psychology of Human Misjudgment."[94]

2. Loss Aversion

Definition: People feel the sting of losses about twice as strongly as they enjoy the thrill of equivalent gains.

Kahneman and Tversky showed this with a simple truth: losing $100 hurts more than gaining $100 feels good.

Why it matters: At the Solve stage, clients are comparing your solution to the "do nothing" option. Upside sounds nice, but it rarely drives action. Highlighting the cost of inaction flips the frame. Once the pain of loss is real, moving forward feels less like risk and more like protection.

Example: "Every quarter this project stalls, you're not just missing upside—you're losing $120K in preventable churn. That's money you're handing to competitors."

Remember: People run faster to avoid loss than to chase gain.

Source: Daniel Kahneman and Amos Tversky, "Prospect Theory: An Analysis of Decision under Risk."[95]

3. Paradox of Choice

Definition: Too many options don't empower people. They overwhelm them.

Barry Schwartz called this the Paradox of Choice: more freedom can actually paralyze action. The fear of choosing wrong stalls decisions before they begin.

Why it matters: In the Solve stage, clients want to feel confident, not confused. Giving them five options might feel thorough, but it backfires. When you narrow the field to two or three well-framed options, you replace doubt with clarity, and clarity unlocks commitment.

Example: "There are two paths: one optimizes for speed, the other for flexibility. Both work. The choice depends on which fits your strategy best."

Remember: More is less.

Source: Barry Schwartz, *The Paradox of Choice: Why More Is Less.*[96]

4. Processing Fluency

Definition: The easier something is to process, the truer it seems.

Psychologists call this processing fluency: when information is simple, structured, and clear, the brain rewards it with trust. If complex or jargon-heavy, the brain flags it as risky.

Why it matters: In the Solve stage, your solution must feel not just smart, but easy to grasp. Complexity creates hesitation. Clarity creates confidence. A clean rollout plan, a three-step framework, or a simple visual removes friction and makes the path forward feel obvious.

Example: "Here's how the rollout works: Phase 1: data alignment. Phase 2: activation. Phase 3: feedback loop. Simple, predictable, proven."

Remember: Simplicity sells.

Source: Rolf Reber, Norbert Schwarz, and Piotr Winkielman, "Processing Fluency and Aesthetic Pleasure: Is Beauty in the Perceiver's Processing Experience?"[97]

5. IKEA Effect

Definition: People value things more when they've had a hand in creating them, even if the result is no better than a ready-made alternative.

Norton, Mochon, and Ariely named this the IKEA Effect. That wobbly bookshelf you built yourself feels priceless compared to the flawless one you bought. The effort isn't just labor. It's ownership.

Why it matters: In the Solve stage, co-creation turns a pitch into a partnership. When clients help shape the solution, even in small ways, it stops being "your" idea and becomes "our" solution. Ownership makes the outcome stickier, more trusted, and far harder to walk away from.

Example: On a recent rollout, instead of delivering a fixed plan, we invited the client's ops lead to tweak the workflow steps. The changes were minor (just renaming phases and shifting one milestone), but the impact was huge. From that point on, he referred to it as our process. He defended it in every leadership meeting because it carried his fingerprints.

Remember: People love what they build.

Source: Michael I. Norton, Daniel Mochon, and Dan Ariely, "The IKEA Effect: When Labor Leads to Love."[98]

Summary of Stage 3: Solve

Everything should be made as simple as possible, but not simpler.[99]

— *Albert Einstein*

In Solve, the client wants answers—but clarity beats complexity. Authority Bias builds trust, Loss Aversion makes inaction costly, and the Paradox of Choice shows that fewer options drive decisions. The best solution isn't just correct—it also feels right.

Stage 4: Vision

Persuasion is not complete when a solution is presented. It becomes powerful only when the client can see themselves using it. Humans act on images of the future. When that image feels real, vivid, and attainable, it creates the pull that drives action.

This stage is where we shift from features to futures, from problem-solving to identity-shaping. And here, heuristics again play a central role. Visualization makes success feel certain. Labels shape identity. Anticipated regret pushes for action. Each one works like a lens, bringing tomorrow into sharper focus.

1. Visualization Heuristic

Definition: When people vividly imagine a future experience, it becomes more emotionally and cognitively real, and therefore more likely to guide their decisions. Mental simulation is not daydreaming; it is rehearsal.

Why it matters: If a client can see themselves already in the successful future state (the smoother process, the faster team, the relieved manager), then the path toward it feels natural, even inevitable. Visualization turns an abstract solution into a lived experience.

Example: Instead of saying, "Our system will improve your efficiency," try: "Within three months: backlog gone, escalations under control, your Monday stand-up actually ends on time. What's the first thing you'd do with that extra breathing room?"

Remember: What the mind can believe, it can achieve.

Source: Lien Pham and Shelley Taylor, "From Thought to Action: Effects of Process-Versus Outcome-Based Mental Simulations on Performance."[100]

2. Goal Gradient Effect

Definition: Motivation increases as people perceive themselves moving closer to a meaningful goal.

Why it matters: In sales, clients often stall because the journey looks endless. But when you highlight how much progress they've already made, and how close they are to the next milestone—energy returns.

Example: "Think about it—you've already done the hardest part: getting your leadership team aligned. Now it's just execution. The next step is straightforward, and once it's done, you'll be 70% of the way there."

Remember: The closer the goal, the stronger the drive.

Source: Ran Kivetz, Oleg Urminsky, and Yuhuang Zheng, "The Goal-Gradient Hypothesis Resurrected: Purchase Acceleration, Illusion of Goal Progress, and Customer Retention." [101]

3. Labeling Effect

Definition: People act in ways that are consistent with the identities they're given.

Why it matters: In sales, assigning a client a role they want to embody (innovator, problem-solver, change agent) can be a powerful nudge. Once named, people naturally align their choices with that identity.

Example: In one deal, a COO had been pushing through resistance from her peers. I told her: "You've been the change-maker here. The one holding the bigger picture when others got stuck in the weeds." From that moment, she fought for the project as if it was proof of her leadership.

Remember: Give people a name they want to live up to.

Source: Daryl J. Bem, "Self-Perception Theory."[102]

4. Sunk Cost Avoidance

Definition: People do not want to see their invested effort and money being wasted.

Why it matters: Your clients have already invested heavily in the process with you: discovery calls, alignment meetings, shared data, and pilot steps. If the project stalls, all of that investment devolves into a sunk cost. But if you position the next step as the payoff, the decision feels like finally cashing in.

Example: In one engagement, a leadership team had already spent months aligning stakeholders, sharing internal data, and feeding insights into our workshops. Instead of letting hesitation creep in, I reframed their position: the hardest work was already done, the foundation was solid, and moving forward meant turning that investment into results.

Remember: People do not want to waste their effort.

Source: Hal Arkes and Catherine Blumer, "The Psychology of Sunk Cost."[103]

5. Anticipated Regret

Definition: People often make choices not by weighing gains, but by imagining the sting of a missed chance. The fear of future regret is one of the strongest motivators for action.

Why it matters: In moments of hesitation, clients picture two futures: one where they acted and moved forward, and one where they stood still. The second vision (explaining to their board why competitors pulled ahead, or why opportunities slipped by) is often unbearable. Anticipated regret transforms inaction from "safe" to risky.

Example: In a strategy session, a CEO wavered on green-lighting a new platform. I asked him to imagine the same conversation a year later, but with two rivals already capturing market share. The thought of explaining to investors why his company lagged was enough to tip the scales. He chose to move, not because the numbers changed, but because the cost of regret became undeniable.

Remember: People forgive mistakes of action; they rarely forgive mistakes of inaction.

Source: Graham Loomes and Robert Sugden, "Regret Theory: An Alternative Theory of Rational Choice Under Uncertainty." [104]

Summary of Stage5: Vision

Whatever the mind can conceive and believe, it can achieve. [105]

— *Napoleon Hill*

In the Vision stage, persuasion moves beyond solving problems—it helps the client see themselves in a future of success. Visualization makes that future vivid and attainable. Once the picture of tomorrow feels real, moving forward becomes the only natural step.

Stage 5: Commit

Commitment must create urgency and inspire immediate action. Every salesperson knows this moment: the client nods, agrees the solution fits, even admits the future looks better with it—and yet, when it comes time to sign, they hesitate. They stall, ask for "more time," or kick the decision to another quarter. The deal is alive, but not moving.

This hesitation isn't about logic. It's about psychology. People want the benefits of progress but fear the cost of choosing. That's why the final stage of persuasion is less about more arguments and more about framing the choice so it feels safe, urgent, and inevitable. Scarcity sharpens attention. Small early commitments create momentum. Clear next steps turn intention into behavior.

The best salespeople don't push harder here. They guide the client across the line in a way that feels natural, even self-driven.

Because when commitment feels like their decision—not your request—hesitation disappears, and action begins.

1. Scarcity Heuristic

Definition: When something feels rare or fleeting, its value rises instantly.

Classic research showed this power. In the "cookie jar" experiment, identical cookies were judged as far more desirable when the jar held only two instead of ten. Scarcity shifts the psychology from "why now?" to "what if I don't?"

Why it matters: At the commit stage, clients often agree in principle but stall in action. Scarcity flips the frame: waiting is no longer neutral, it's a loss.

Example: In one deal, a platform rollout stalled until we made one fact clear: early adopters would lock in access to a capability competitors couldn't get later. Suddenly, the question wasn't whether to commit. It was how quickly they could secure their spot.

Remember: Scarcity creates urgency.

Source: Stephen Worchel, Jerry Lee, and Akanbi Adewole, "Effects of Supply and Demand on Ratings of Object Value."[106]

2. Hyperbolic Discounting

Definition: People give more weight to rewards they can get now than to larger ones they'll receive later. The near-term payoff always feels more real. Ainslie's 1975 paper argues that people systematically choose smaller, immediate rewards over larger, delayed ones. Highlighting immediate wins makes the decision feel rewarding right away.

Why it matters: At the commit stage, clients don't just want to hear about ROI three years out. They want to know what changes next month.

Example: In a transformation project, we didn't lead with the five-year efficiency model. Instead, we showed that in the first 30 days, reporting time would be cut in half.

Remember: We overvalue the present and undervalue the future.

Source: George Ainslie, "Specious Reward: A Behavioral Theory of Impulsiveness and Impulse Control."[107]

3.   Foot-in-the-Door Technique (The First Yes)

Definition: Saying yes to a small, harmless request dramatically increases the chance of saying yes to a bigger one later.

Freedman and Fraser's 1966 study proved this vividly: people who agreed to place a tiny sign in their window were far more likely to later accept a giant billboard on their lawn.

Why it matters: The first yes breaks resistance, builds comfort, and makes consistency the default.

Example: "I understand a full rollout feels like a big leap. How about we start with a short, two-hour discovery session with your leads? It gives you a feel for how we work."

Remember: The first yes unlocks the next.

Source: Jonathan Freedman and Scott Fraser, "Compliance Without Pressure: The Foot-in-the-Door Technique."[108]

4. Escalation of Commitment

Definition: Once people commit to a course of action, they feel compelled to remain consistent, often escalating their involvement rather than reversing course.

Barry Staw's research shows that commitments create momentum. He found that reversing a decision feels like a public failure, whereas escalating commitment feels like natural progress.

Why it matters: Clients rarely undo what they've already agreed to; instead, they deepen their investment to stay consistent with their prior choices and protect credibility.

Example: A client who agreed to a limited pilot quickly shifted from "testing the waters" to pushing for full deployment. The act of committing to the pilot created its own gravity, escalating their commitment until expansion felt not like a new decision, but the natural continuation of what was already started.

Remember: Commitment creates escalation.

Source: Barry Staw, "The Escalation of Commitment: An Update and Appraisal."[109]

5. If-Then Planning

Definition: People are more likely to act when they tie a decision to a specific if-then condition: if this happens, then I will do that.

Peter Gollwitzer's research showed that if-then plans dramatically increase follow-through by turning vague intentions into concrete commitments.

Why it matters: In sales, this principle lets you move past hesitation. Instead of asking for a leap of faith, you invite the client to agree on a clear trigger for action.

Example: "If the pilot delivers the savings you're aiming for, then will you move ahead with the full rollout?"

Remember: If – Then commitment.

Source: Peter Gollwitzer, "Implementation Intentions: Strong Effects of Simple Plans." [110]

Summary of Stage 5: Commit

This is the moment of truth. The client sees the future, believes in the solution, and yet their pen hovers. Why? Because committing is never just about logic. It's about fear of loss, of risk, of being wrong. That's where psychology becomes your ally. Scarcity shifts the question from *"why now?"* to *"what if I miss out?"* A quick win brings the future rushing into the present. A single small yes cascades into bigger ones, and once a step is taken, momentum makes retreat unthinkable. The best closers don't pressure. They choreograph.

ABC — Always Be Closing. [111]

— *David Mamet*

On a Personal Note,

Entire industries now thrive on capturing and monetizing our attention, most visibly through social media and digital advertising. Billions are poured into conventional media to steer public opinion, shaping narratives that serve political or commercial agendas. Some of this is driven by honest idealists, others by hostile foreign powers. Whatever the source, these industries rank among the most successful of our time. The polarized democracies of the early 21st century stand as undeniable proof of just how powerful heuristics can be when applied at scale.

And yet, I choose to believe in something deeper: that human beings ultimately strive for self-agency. Beyond persuasion and manipulation, our most important decisions are guided by genuine Inspiration and Motivation: the pursuit of meaning and the drive to achieve it.

Summary of Chapter 3: Persuasion

Persuasion is not as enduring as Motivation, and certainly not as powerful as Inspiration. That is why it is addressed last in this book. The strongest way to drive business is still to work with customers who believe in our solutions and see us as co-visionaries. It is also powerful to understand and fulfill their deepest needs: technical, financial, and emotional. That is the path of Motivation.

Without doubt, those are the best drivers to grow our business!

Yet, as professionals and as human beings, we cannot neglect the truth that people are not always rational. We also cannot ignore the reality that the way a message is presented shapes the decisions people make. That is why we should treat heuristics as practical tools to move a deal forward or to strengthen our position against competitors. We use them as part of our skill set as sales professionals, and we should never forget that our customers and competitors use them as well. Heuristics are a powerful force, scientifically proven to guide decisions and change perceptions. When applied wisely, they give us a much greater chance of winning any deal. This is why I urge you to remember the Persuasion Flow and use the right heuristics at the right time.

The Persuasion techniques are not a magic trick. We must always remember that we are dealing with highly capable people: COOs, CFOs, VPs of R&D, and CEOs. In many cases, they are smarter, better informed, and better resourced than we are. They reached their positions by making rational decisions again and again, decisions grounded in genuine Inspiration from their goals and Motivation to achieve them. Therefore, we must use these techniques thoughtfully, carefully, and with the utmost respect for the buyer's intellect.

As in the famous quote often attributed to Abraham Lincoln (though originally traced to Jacques Abbadie):

> *You can fool a few people, or fool everyone in some places and for some time, but you cannot fool everyone everywhere and for all time.*[112]

— *Jacques Abbadie*

The Five Stages of Persuasion & 25 Heuristics

To help us remember this complex structure and the 25 heuristics, I've prepared a short summary as a quick reference. A cheat sheet. Keep it close: on your desk or in your notebook. It is a practical tool to guide you in applying the Persuasion Flow with confidence and precision.

Flow: Connect → Frame → Solve → Vision → Commit

Stage 1: Connect: Build emotional connection and trust

- **Halo Effect**: Create a first impression of warmth and calm.
- **Social Proof**: Show that others already choose you.
- **In-Group Bias**: Build trust by being seen as "one of us."
- **Reciprocal Self-Disclosure**: Share openly, and they will too.
- **Affect Heuristic**: Make the interaction feel positive and rewarding.

Stage 2: Frame: Reshape how the client sees reality

- **Anchoring Bias**: Set the first anchor with your numbers.
- **Narrative Relabeling**: Use a professional negative label for the rival's solution.
- **False Uniqueness**: Reveal that what feels unique is common.
- **Framing Effect**: Present the current situation as a loss to be avoided.
- **Story Bias**: Data fades, but stories stick—create a new narrative.

Stage 3: Solve: Present clear and credible solution

- **Authority Bias**: Bring in experts to deliver the message.
- **Loss Aversion**: Frame your solution as preventing a loss.
- **Paradox of Choice**: Offer 2–3 clear options, not too many.
- **Processing Fluency**: Make your solution simple and easy to grasp.
- **IKEA Effect**: Co-create; people value what they help build.

Stage 4: Vision: Help the client imagine a successful future

- **Visualization Heuristic**: Let them imagine their life with the problem solved.

- **Goal Gradient**: Show how close they are to achieving success.

- **Labeling Effect**: Give them a positive label they will live up to.

- **Sunk Cost Avoidance**: Remind them of the effort already invested.

- **Anticipated Regret**: Use fear of missed opportunity to drive action.

Stage 5: Commit: Turn intent into action

- **Scarcity Heuristic**: Emphasize rarity: what is scarce feels valuable.

- **Hyperbolic Discounting**: Highlight quick wins now, not just future ROI.

- **Foot-in-the-Door**: Start with a small yes to unlock bigger ones.

- **Escalation of Commitment**: Build momentum through cumulative steps.

- **If–Then Planning**: Tie the next step to a clear and specific trigger.

CHAPTER 4

The Socratic Dialogue:
Coaching Salespeople

Scene 1: "I Did Everything Right and Still Lost"

The office was almost dark.

The open space looked like a paused movie: rows of black screens, pushed-back chairs, half-empty water bottles no one would ever claim. Only one small meeting room was still lit. Inside, a laptop glowed with an untouched forecast spreadsheet.

The Salesperson stared at the screen as if it owed him money.

The door opened with a soft click. The Regional Sales Manager (RSM) leaned in, jacket over his arm.

RSM: You're still here.

Salesperson: Apparently.

RSM: Strong statement. Very data-driven.

(He steps in, drops his jacket on the back of a chair, and sits opposite.)

RSM: So. What's the name of the corpse?

Salesperson: The Meridian account. The big one. Eighteen months of calls, workshops, pilots, internal champions, deal reviews, legal approvals... Gone.

RSM: "Gone" as in...?

Salesperson: As in: "After careful consideration, we've decided to continue with our existing supplier. Thank you for your efforts."

You know, that "thank you for your efforts" part really adds insult. Like a condolence card for a deal.

RSM: Ah, the classic corporate breakup: "It's not you, it's procurement."

(*He folds his hands, calm.*)

RSM: All right. Give me your version.

Salesperson: My version?

RSM: Yes. The one you've been looping in your head for the last two hours. The "Director's Cut."

Salesperson: Fine.
    I did everything right.
    Discovery: deep.
    Stakeholders: mapped.
    KPIs: understood.
    Business case: very competitive.
    Technical evaluation: successful.
    Security: approved.
    Legal: halfway to the finish line.

I followed the process. I was the process. And then procurement swooped in, the CTO got nervous, everyone remembered their "trusted relationship" with the old vendor, and suddenly sticking with the past became "strategic."

RSM: So, in the official story:

    you = competent,

    they = conservative,

    fate = unfair.

Salesperson: You forgot "procurement = evil," but yes, that's the summary.

RSM: And what's the emotional diagnosis? What are you feeling?

Salesperson: Right now? Tired and humiliated. Like I studied for the exam, wrote all the answers, and the teacher decided to grade handwriting instead. And there's this small voice saying: "If this is what 'good process' gets you, maybe next time just discount early, send the deck, and save yourself the cardio."

RSM: Mm. That brings back memories. The 4th Quarter of 2015. I was sitting in that exact chair, staring at the Oracle contract. It was a 2.5-million-dollar deal. I had already put it in the forecast as "Committed." I had even booked the victory dinner for the team. Then, at 4:30 PM on a Friday, I got a three-line email from their procurement. They weren't just delaying; they were pivoting to a competitor because of a "strategic realignment." I didn't go home that night. I sat there until the cleaning crew came in at midnight, staring at the spreadsheet, trying to mathematically find a way to hit my yearly target without them.

I couldn't.

You're at the standard fork in the road. There are two very popular explanations for a lost deal:

"They're idiots."

"I'm an idiot."

Both feel honest. Neither is useful.

Salesperson: Great. So not only did I lose, but I also chose the wrong coping mechanism.

RSM: Let's try the third option. More painful, but more interesting.

(*He reaches over and gently closes the laptop. The forecast disappears.*)

RSM: Forget CRM fairy tales. Walk me through what you actually did on this deal. Step by step. Human version, not pipeline version.

Salesperson: Okay. First call: classic B2B.

I mapped their pain—delays, manual work, and integration hell. I asked about budgets and deadlines. I gathered requirements, drew diagrams, did the whole "tell me about your challenges" ritual.

Then I built a business case: "If you keep going like this, it costs you X. If you switch, you save Y. Here's the ROI slide with the impressive green arrows."

We did a proof of concept and it worked. I lined up references. I handled objections, nudged next steps, chased internal approvals. Textbook Motivation and Persuasion.

RSM: Textbook Motivation and Persuasion.

Salesperson: Yes. That's what we train on, right? Align with their why, understand their Motivation, answer their needs. Use Persuasion to drive the decision!

RSM: No. That's surface Motivation and a lot of presenting.

That's not Persuasion.

Salesperson: Oh, come on. I framed ROI, anticipated push-backs, guided them through the stages. If that's not persuasion, then what is? Hypnosis?

RSM: Persuasion isn't "talking harder." Persuasion is designing how a decision will feel the right thing to do. You didn't design their decision. You threw arguments at their anxiety and hoped something would stick.

Salesperson: So now I'm doing hope-based selling. Wonderful.

RSM: Look, I'm not saying you're bad. If anything, you're good enough to lose in the final round. Most reps never even get there. I'm saying you're doing what almost every competent B2B salesperson does:

> You chase visible pain.

> You build a rational case around it.

> You do a strong show-and-tell.

Then you pray that fear, habit, and internal politics will magically behave. When they don't, you blame fear, habit, and internal politics.

Salesperson: You say that like those aren't real. They live in every meeting I've ever attended.

RSM: They're real. They just aren't random.

They are what you get when three layers are misaligned. And you only touched the middle one.

Salesperson: Here we go. The Three-Layer sermon.

RSM: Yes, here we go. Pretend for one minute you haven't already decided it's bullshit. Describe your job in one sentence. Your version, not HR's.

Salesperson: I find the pain, I show the value, I close the deal. That's the job.

RSM: Good. That's Layer Two.

Salesperson: Layer Two of what?

RSM: Of this.

(*He pulls a notepad closer and writes three words, one under the other, in big letters.*)

Inspiration

Motivation

Persuasion

(*He turns the pad, so it faces the Salesperson.*)

RSM: Here's the fantasy: Sales read about this model in training. Everyone nods: "Yes, yes, Inspiration, Motivation, Persuasion, very deep." Then they go back to doing exactly what they did before and logging it neatly in the CRM.

In their heads:

Inspiration = "Marketing buzzwords on the website."

Motivation = "I asked what hurts and how much it costs."

Persuasion = "I talked a lot and asked for the order."

Reality:

They touch only the polite part of Motivation—the stuff that's safe to say out loud.

They do almost no real Persuasion. They present; they don't design. And they completely ignore Inspiration.

Salesperson: I don't ignore Inspiration. I just... don't see how to use it without sounding fake. Whenever someone starts a meeting with, "We're here to support your noble mission," I die a little inside. And so do they.

RSM: Good. You should die inside. That's not Inspiration. That's flattery with extra syllables. If you walk into a boardroom and say, "We read your website and we are so inspired,"

you are announcing, "We did basic homework and now we will emotionally manipulate you."

You deserve to lose.

Salesperson: Exactly. That's what I'm avoiding. I don't want to be an inspirational clown.

RSM: Then don't. But pretending Inspiration doesn't exist because some people abuse the language is like refusing to talk about money because some people run Ponzi schemes.

Let's clean this up.

Inspiration is the customer's "who we are" and "what we strive to achieve." It's not slogans; it's customer identity. Motivation is what the actual people in the room need, fear, and want right now. Not just what they say to look professional, but what they don't say to avoid looking weak.

Persuasion is how you shape the path from here to there: what feels safe, what feels good, what feels like "us." You worked hard on the middle line, and even there, mostly on the CRM friendly parts. You never really engaged with the top line. You did not reveal their suppressed needs and fears. And your "Persuasion" was mostly you repeating, "this makes sense," slightly louder.

Salesperson: So you're saying I didn't lose because of price, or procurement, or politics... I lost because I didn't... inspire them?

RSM: No. I'm saying you lost because of three things.

First, you never really helped them answer "Why change at all?" Not "why save some dollars" or "why improve turnaround time." I mean:

"Why does this change move us closer to who we want to be as a company?" You kept it at operational goals. You never connected our solution to their existential goal—the big story they're trying to live out.

Second, you only scratched the surface of their needs. The polite, explicit needs. You missed the C-level suppressed needs—the things they'd never put in a slide or an email. The fears and desires they only admit to a friend over a drink:

"I don't want to be exposed as all talk."

"I want to leave a legacy, not just a budget."

"If this fails, it's my head on the wall."

Those are needs too.

Third, you didn't design the decision path. A decision isn't a single moment; it's a sequence. Did you reframe the situation so the current state clearly looked like a problem that must be solved?

Did you help them visualize success after implementing our solution—what changes in their world, concretely?

How many small commitments did you collect along the way, or did you just aim for the order?

You didn't guide the customers through their feelings. You just hoped logic would overpower gravity.

In most cases, "stick with what we know" will win nine times out of ten. Not because your solution is bad, but because the status quo has home-court advantage.

Salesperson: Because staying where they are feels like a safer mistake.

RSM: Exactly. If they move and it goes badly, someone gets blamed by name. If they stay and it goes badly, everyone shrugs and says, "market conditions." Unless something stronger pulls them forward, they don't move.

Salesperson: And that "something stronger" is... these three aligned?

RSM: Now you're using the expensive words correctly. When:

Their Inspiration is clearly at stake!

Their real Motivation—including the ugly, political, human bits—is addressed, and your Persuasion makes the first step feel safer than doing nothing, then a big, risky decision suddenly becomes the obvious one.

Salesperson: Okay, but be honest: most of us don't work like that. We don't walk around thinking, "Hmm, what is their existential identity conflict today?"

RSM: Of course not. That's why you're here at 20:47 with a dead latte and a dead deal. I'm not trying to turn you into a philosopher in a blazer. I want something simpler and nastier.

When you think about a deal from now on, I want you to be able to say, with a straight face:

I know what story drives this company.

I know what each C-level player privately needs or fears.

I have planned the path, so it feels like the least dangerous way to go.

And I know where they are on that path. Right now, on this Meridian deal, can you honestly tick those three boxes?

Salesperson: No. I can tell you their backlog, their integration issues, their overtime numbers. I can quote my own slides by heart. But if you ask me:

"What does their CEO secretly fear will be exposed if they fail?"

"What keeps their CTO awake that he didn't dare admit in front of his team?"

I've got nothing.

RSM: Good. That's clarity. Painful clarity, but still clarity. Tonight, we're not fixing your forecast. We're doing something more dangerous to your ego and more useful to your future. We're going to autopsy this deal through these three words. Inspiration, Motivation and Persuasion.

Then we'll look at a live one and see where it's already bleeding. By the end, if you still call what you're doing "Persuasion," it will be because you're designing decisions— not just narrating slides.

Salesperson: And if we find out I've been doing it wrong for five years?

RSM: Then you're ahead of the curve. Most people do it wrong for twenty and call it "experience."

(The Salesperson snorts despite himself.)

RSM: So. Shall we start with the part where you "did everything right"?

(The room feels smaller now: laptop closed, cold coffee ignored, and on the table between them, three handwritten words that suddenly feel heavier than any forecast.)

Scene 2: Inspiration You Never Say Out Loud

The next morning, the office looked like the same movie, but with better lighting.

Same small meeting room. Different coffee cups. The forecast spreadsheet was gone; in its place, a notebook lay open, blank except for one word written in big letters at the top:

Inspiration

The Salesperson walked in, handed over a coffee, and sat down with a sigh.

RSM: This is the layer you skipped completely.

Salesperson: I didn't skip it. I just... didn't do a full TED Talk about their purpose in life.

RSM: Good. TED Talks lose deals. What you did is what most reps do: you skimmed the website, memorized the tagline, and called it "understanding their why."

Salesperson: Well, yeah. I read the "About" page. I know their mission. That's Inspiration, isn't it?

RSM: No. That's marketing. Remember the book? Inspiration isn't marketing. It's the strongest drive—spiritual, meaning-ful, often transcendental. It's the force that moves people despite comfort and fear, not because of them.

Salesperson: Still not seeing what I do with it in a meeting.

RSM: Good. Let's start with what you were supposed to do and didn't. Remember Chapter 1? The workflow?

Step One—Investigation for Inspiration.

Step Two—Ask Meaningful Questions.

Salesperson: Of course. I read the book *Start with Why* twice. During the customer meeting, I introduce myself and ask, "So what's your 'why'?" Then I nod very wisely and smile.

RSM: That's not Step One. That's Step "How to get kicked out of the account in one meeting." Step One is:

Learn what problem they exist to solve.

Read what the CEO and CTO say in interviews, shareholder letters, talks.

Understand how their products help their customers.

That's investigation.

That's where you start to smell their meaning, not just their marketing.

Salesperson: Okay, guilty. I do about 20% of that on a good day.

RSM: Fine. But the real missed piece is Step Two—Ask Meaningful Questions. That's where Frankl comes in. Logotherapy. Existential questions. You don't have to say "existential vacuum" in a meeting, but you do have to ask something deeper than "What are your challenges this year?"

(He flips to a clean page and writes at the top:)

Phase 1: Why Do We Exist?

RSM: These questions aren't my invention. They're from the framework.

"Beyond financial success, what significant problem does your business exist to solve, and why does it matter?"
(He lets the words hang for a second.)

RSM: That's not fluffy. That's precise. That's Frankl in a suit.

Salesperson: If I ask that in a first meeting, won't they just look at me like, "Who invited the philosopher?"

RSM: Depends on how you show up. If you show you actually understand their world, this question feels natural. Leaders are used to talking about this—just not with vendors. Let's try it. You're you. I'm Meridian's CEO. Ask me properly.

Salesperson: Okay. Let me try:

"Beyond revenue and profitability, what significant problem does Meridian really exist to solve—and why is that problem important to you?"

RSM: Good. Now watch. As CEO, I might say:

"There are many cracks in the healthcare system. Coordination is a joke. We're trying to make sure a patient is treated as a whole person, not as three disconnected files."

Salesperson: And what if they don't want to answer?

RSM: You don't force it. You move on. But if you never ask, you'll never even know if there's anything to work with. The second question should be:

"If your company ceased to exist tomorrow, who would miss it most, and why?"

Same thing. You're not being poetic. You're asking: "Who depends on you being alive?"

Salesperson: So, I'm basically asking, "If you die, who comes to the funeral?"

RSM: Exactly. If nobody notices, that's one kind of customer. If a whole ecosystem panics, that's another. You want to partner with the second kind.

Salesperson: Okay, that one I like. Dark, but useful.

RSM: There's a third one in Phase 1: "What conventional belief or outdated practice does your company challenge?"

That's your rebel question. It tells you whether they're here to maintain the status quo or break it. The point of these three questions is simple:

What challenge do you live for?

Who would bleed if you disappeared?

What bullshit in your industry are you refusing to accept?

That's Inspiration, in simple language.

Salesperson: Fine. But I can't just bombard them with existential questions one after another.

RSM: Correct. This is not an intake session in therapy. You weave them in. Maybe in a first deep meeting, you ask just one: "If your company ceased to exist tomorrow, who would miss it most?"

If the answer has life in it—emotion, specifics—you stay there a little. If it's dead, you don't drill. You move back to normal business.

Salesperson: So that's Phase 1: "Why do we exist?" And then?

RSM: Then comes Phase 2—Bridging Vision and Execution.

Because meaning without action is just inspirational posters. You should ask:

"What are the critical areas where your company must execute to stay true to its purpose?"

This is gold. Once they answer, they're telling you exactly where failure would feel like a betrayal of their identity, not just a bad quarter. If they say: "For us, it's patient safety and real-time data sharing. If we fail there, our whole mission is a joke."

Boom. That's where your solution really matters. If we can address it, we might win the business.

Salesperson: Okay, that I see. It tells me where my product must land to be strategic, not just "nice-to-have."

RSM: Exactly. Next one:

"Where do you see the biggest gaps between your company's purpose and its current execution?"

That's the Inspiration Gap question, written in polite business terms. This is often where their existing vendor is falling short. You're basically asking: "What are the weaknesses of your current solution that are existential for you?"

If they trust you, this is where the real story comes out.

Salesperson: And then the innovation one, right?

RSM: Right. "How does innovation play a role in turning your company's vision into reality?"

If they talk big about challenging conventions but treat innovation like a budget line to be minimized, you've learned something.

Salesperson: So Phase 1 is "Why do you exist?" Phase 2 is "How does that actually show up—or fail—in real life?"

RSM: Exactly. Now, notice what we're not doing:

> We're not saying, "Tell me about your Inspiration."
>
> We're not reciting Genesis or Dante at them.

We did the theory at home.

In the meeting, we ask sharp business questions about the practical side of meaning.

Salesperson: And then at the end we have that summary question, right?

RSM: Yes:

"How can our partnership improve to better bring your company's mission to life?"

That's the moment where you stop being a salesperson and start being "someone who is willing to share responsibility for the mission."

Salesperson: Sounds risky.

RSM: It is. That's why almost nobody asks it. But when you've already done Phase 1 and Phase 2—when you've shown you understand their "why" and their execution gaps. It sounds logical. It shows that you really care and can actually help.

Salesperson: Okay, but be practical with me. What do you want me to do in my next big meeting?

RSM: Simple. You've got, what, three strategic meetings next week?

Salesperson: Four.

RSM: Pick one. The most important. For that meeting, do real investigation beforehand. 30 minutes more than you usually do. Not browsing but reading. In the meeting itself, ask one Phase 1 question and one Phase 2 question. For example:

"If your company ceased to exist tomorrow, who would miss it most, and why?"

"Where do you see the biggest gaps between your company's purpose and its current execution?"

At the end, ONLY if the conversation went deep and trust is there, ask the summary question:

"How can our partnership improve to better bring your company's mission to life?"

That's it. No new slides. No quotes from Nietzsche. Just these questions.

Salesperson: And if they say, "Look, we just need to reduce integration costs by 15%. Can you do it or not?"

RSM: Then you meet them there. In the next interaction, you build trust and share your own thoughts and experiences. Then, try again to elevate the conversation.

Salesperson: You realize this is a lot more interesting than "Tell me what issues you have with your current system," right?

RSM: That's the point. You should genuinely care about their mission. You should want to help them fulfill their purpose. You can't fake it; they'll feel it.

Salesperson: So, Inspiration is not something I repeat with big words. It must move me, too—we both need to feel it.

RSM: Exactly. Think of Inspiration. Use logotherapy questions. Become their partner by caring about their goal. Find ways our products can support that purpose.

Next time, we'll go to the middle layer: the parts they won't say when the whole team is in the room.

That's Motivation.

(The Salesperson looks down at their notepad. The standard, rigid checklist of 'Pain Points' and 'Budget' has been entirely crossed out. Beneath it, written in bold, urgent letters, is a single question: *What is their purpose?*)

Scene 3: The Needs They Won't Put on a Slide

The cafeteria was almost empty. Just the soft hum of the coffee machine and the occasional spoon against porcelain.

The Salesperson sat with a tray—coffee, something that used to be a sandwich, and a notebook already open. The RSM arrived with nothing but his mug and a pen, dropped into the chair opposite, and drew 5 big waves across the page.

Salesperson: We're doing surfing lessons now?

RSM: This is Maslow.

Salesperson: Pretty sure Maslow was a pyramid in every training I've ever seen.

RSM: In PowerPoint, yes. In reality, Maslow never presented human needs as a pyramid. In Maslow's view, needs rise and fall. They overlap. Higher needs have greater magnitude; basic needs are smaller but must be addressed first. Picture them as five waves, each larger than the last. And just like human needs, the waves overlap.

Salesperson: OK. I can see that.

RSM: You wanted to understand why you "did everything right" and still lost, remember? Today is Motivation Day.

Salesperson: Here we go. This is the part where you tell me I must be a psychologist. Read childhood trauma through Zoom. Look, I do not have time for this...

RSM: Relax. I don't need you to diagnose anyone. I just need you to stop calling "irrational behavior" irrational. When a smart C-level does something that makes no sense on your slide, it makes perfect sense in their head. That's a suppressed need. Our job in sales is simple: uncover what they really need and see where we can honestly help. Suppressed needs are still "needs."

Salesperson: Listen, they don't reveal their "needs." C-levels don't sit there and say, "I'm secretly afraid of losing status, please help." They talk about governance, compliance, and budget.

RSM: Exactly. That's why we have an entire chapter about it. Needs don't walk in naked. They show up wearing business language.

Salesperson: And I'm supposed to see through the clothes? What am I, an X-ray machine? A wizard?

RSM: No. You're a pattern spotter. As all humans are. You have two places to look:

Field A—Logic: The pattern of their past decisions.

Field B—Behavior: The tone, timing, body language.

Salesperson: Look, you don't know how tough it is out there. People are working from home, joining conference calls in a T-shirt, or with cameras off while they're driving. Reading body language is impossible now. And honestly, even when you can see them, it's not reliable—it's situational. Reading body language does not work. It works in textbooks. In real life, C-level leaders know how to handle themselves. It's impossible to read them.

RSM: You are right. It is tough. Let's start with something simple in Field A, contradictions. Remember that VP who told you: "We need a bold, innovative leap... but we absolutely cannot take any risk."

You laughed, because it sounded like: "We want a fast rocket that cannot leave the ground."

Salesperson: Yeah. I remember.

RSM: You treated it as stupidity. It wasn't stupidity. It was fear colliding with ambition. His expressed need was Esteem—"I want to be the hero who brings innovation." His suppressed need was Safety—"If this blows up, they hang me in the boardroom." He did express his fear of failure to you. You just did not listen.

Salesperson: Okay, but what do I do with that? I'm not going to say, "Wow, it seems like you are suppressing your fear of failure."

RSM: Good. Please don't.

You say something like: "I hear you want a serious innovation leap, and at the same time you can't afford visible failure. Can you walk me through how you balance those two internally with your teams?"

You're not decoding his soul. You're adjusting your solution to his needs, based on what he is doing.

Salesperson: And he'll just... open up?

RSM: Sometimes he'll talk. Sometimes he'll deflect. Either way, now you know: this deal cannot be framed only as "innovation." It must also be framed as career safety. If you don't know what your C-level is secretly afraid of, you don't understand the deal.

Salesperson: Yes. You told me that yesterday.

RSM: Another classic pattern of a Logic irrationality is projection.

Salesperson: Right. In this case, I'd say that, according to Carl Jung, the customer failed to integrate his own shadow. This leads him to resentment and blaming others. When external factors resonate with parts of his personality he dislikes (his shadow), it causes resentment and antisocial behavior. And since he's not mature enough to integrate the dark sides of his personality, he blames the world.

RSM: OK... doctor. Let's save Jung for therapy.

In our world, projection just means he's covering himself: *"It's everyone's fault but mine."*

Projection is when they push all the blame outside: "It wasn't us; the previous vendor couldn't deliver."

"The market shifted unpredictably." "Legal blocked everything." Of course, some of that can be true. But when everything is about other people's failures, it usually means: "If I admit it's me, they'll take my bonus—or my chair." They're protecting themselves by exporting guilt.

Salesperson: So, if a CIO says, "Our old vendor totally screwed us," I shouldn't just jump in with, "Yes, they're terrible and we're the good guys".

RSM: Exactly. If you join the blame party, you miss the point. It's a trap: you'll eventually "fail" in the same way the other vendor had. And now that he's been burned once, the CIO will be far more careful—he might pull out at the last moment just to avoid being blamed again.

Try this instead:

"Sounds like you had a painful experience there. If we work together, what would you want done differently this time—on both sides?"

You acknowledge the story, then steer it toward shared responsibility and the next step—so you can design a solution that fits both his architecture and his scars. Inside your head, you note:

"This person is terrified of repeating a visible failure. My value proposition must scream 'low blame-risk', not just 'better features'."

RSM: Another Logic indicator you'll see in complex deals is Role Shifting.

Salesperson: You mean when my champion disappears and suddenly, I get a calendar invite from "someone new who'll be owning this from now on"?

RSM: Exactly. On paper, it sounds harmless: "We've had some internal changes. From now on, Isabella will own this project." In reality, it often means one of two things: Priorities shifted due to market pressure or a competing offer. Someone higher up wants to redefine the goal and take ownership.

Salesperson: Okay, but what do you want me to do? I don't control their org chart.

RSM: You don't control the org chart, but you do control your focus. When you hear "Isabella will own this," your first thought should be: "Something political just moved above my current altitude."

The worst move is to build rapport with Isabella and behave as if nothing has changed. What you actually want to do is follow the center of gravity of the decision: "I see the project ownership has moved—totally understand. It might make sense to bring your senior leadership into one aligned discussion, so you're not carrying this alone. The GM of our business unit has been wanting to meet your CTO for some time—I'll work on arranging that meeting."

Salesperson: So I don't just charm Isabella, win her over, and carry on? Too bad… that's the one thing I'm really good at.

RSM: You do build trust with Isabella—but you don't stop there. If you keep operating at the old level, they'll make the real decision above you and without you. You must be talking with the real decision-maker. That's your job.

Salesperson: Right. Otherwise, I'm just wining and dining Isabella while someone else decides my fate.

RSM: Exactly. Now let's talk about what we can learn from behavior—body language and tone. First one: elevated pitch and nervous laughter. You've heard this: "No, no, no, we're not *that* worried about downtime, haha… I mean, obviously we can't go offline, but… heh… it'll be fine."

The words say: "*Not a big deal.*"

The voice says: "*I really hope nothing explodes.*"

Salesperson: Weird laughs might just mean they're shy.

RSM: Sometimes, yes. But not always. When you hear the tone jump up at the end of the sentence and they laugh it off, that's a flag. They're trying to minimize the topic verbally while their nervous system is doing the opposite.

That usually signals a safety issue. I'd slow down and address that before moving to another topic:

"Okay, that makes sense. But if something did go wrong here, how can we protect you from the impact?" Now you're giving their fear a safe place to land, without embarrassing them.

RSM: The second behavioral cue is lip compression and face-touching. If you see the CFO's lips press into a thin line, or a hand goes to the face, it means he has a negative thought he isn't sharing.

Salesperson: Yeah, I've seen that. I usually assume, "Okay, they're just thinking."

RSM: Sometimes they are. But often, lip compression and face touching indicate a negative reaction to what you say. As they do not want to share it with you, this is not the time to ask about it. You should move to another subject, build trust and only then revisit this subject again, hoping they'll feel comfortable enough to share what they did not like.

Salesperson: Got it. A few months ago, you spoke about frequency *in a meeting*. What does it mean? Is it about talking too fast?

RSM: No. It is the frequency of topic. The number of times they revisited the same topic in the meeting. It's a strong indicator that they have some anxiety around it.

For example, during a meeting the COO asks you:

"Where is your support center located?"

"How quickly do you respond to critical support tickets?"

"What's your SLA for a system shutdown?"

"Who do we call at 2 a.m.?"

If that theme keeps coming back, that's not curiosity. That's anxiety.

Salesperson: Right. If someone mentions it once, it's a requirement. If they mention it seven times in one hour, it's a fear. Okay—so frequency of a topic in a conversation. Got it. It means I must address it clearly in my value proposition.

RSM: Exactly.

Salesperson: Cool. I feel like I can suddenly see the matrix. Instead of getting emotional and blaming customers, I can understand their motives. From their point of view, their irrational behavior does make sense. From now on, when things feel odd, I will look for patterns in the customer's actions and behavior. This is empowering. I can't wait to try it!

RSM: Hold your horses. I am glad that you are excited. To win, it is not enough to understand the situation, you also need planning and execution. Remember the last part of the Motivation chapter? Turning needs into actions? Deal Plan? Value Proposition?

(*He flips the notebook and draws a table.*)

Stakeholder | Role | Expressed Needs | Suppressed Needs | Our Message | Messenger | Timing

RSM: This is your Deal Plan.

Let's pick a real account... Name a deal.

Salesperson: InTECH. Industrial IoT. Complex, political, fun in a painful way.

RSM: Good. Stakeholder one. Your advocate inside InTECH?

Salesperson: The Product Owner. He's my day-to-day guy and wants usability.

RSM: Expressed needs: "Usability." Suppressed need?

(*Silence.*)

Salesperson: He shared with me over lunch that his team is burned out. His wife just had their third child, so he's working fewer hours while the workload on his team is exploding. He is afraid that someone will leave for a competitor. Every time that we are discussing our solution, he becomes nervous. He asks a lot of questions about the overhead and integration.

RSM: Good observation. He's lower in the org. What hits him first?

Salesperson: Workload. Burnout. Fear his team will hate him if he brings in something heavy.

RSM: Exactly. Safety and belonging.

So, our message to him is not: "Our platform is powerful."

 It's: "Fast deployment, minimal disruption, training that makes your team's life easier. Less work!"

And the messenger is not you alone. It's your application engineer—the one who can show screens, workflows, migration plans.

Next stakeholder.

Salesperson: COO. Big influence. Talks innovation, efficiency, scale.

RSM: And under the water?

Salesperson: He just joined the company. He comes from Cyber Security and has limited understanding of the technical side of Industrial IoT. He took the lead on that project two months ago. He asks too many questions and pushes the real experts aside.

RSM: So, Esteem and Belonging at C-level. He wants to show his peers that he can drive large projects and champion change. He is not from their technical background, so he has much to prove to the C-level team and the board. Your message should be: "This project makes you the one who brought both innovation *and* risk mitigation." Messenger?

Salesperson: Probably not just me. We need somebody strategic to make the COO feel important.

RSM: Right. You bring the Product Manager from San Diego. He can talk strategy, roadmaps, risk management peer-to-peer.

Next.

Salesperson: CFO.

Officially: ROI, cost control.

Unofficially: Fear of missing the financial forecast, again. This will probably be the last time for him. In Q1 2025, InTech's revenue was okay. But their operational margin was much lower than expected. Every time that I raise the subject of moving to our system, the CFO becomes sarcastic.

RSM: You read their Q1 2025 communication and analyst comments? I'm impressed! So, the suppression is safety.

I can help you with this case. We will prepare a proposal with fixed rates for next 3 years. This will give him certainty about the expenses and help him to manage operational margin.

Salesperson: OK. Thank you.

RSM: So, in terms of timing, I think we need the buy-in of the product manager first. Next would be to win over the COO. If we do, the COO will pitch it to the C-level. At this stage, the CFO will have objections that I can address with a fixed-rate proposal. What do you think?

Salesperson: I think we have a Deal Plan and Value Proposition.

RSM: Not yet. Please prepare a detailed Deal Plan with the following columns:

Stakeholder | Role | Expressed Needs | Suppressed Needs | Our Message | Messenger | Timing

We also need a Value Proposition presentation addressing the expressed and suppressed needs of the stakeholders. Please schedule a 1-hour meeting with the account team to review the Deal Plan and the resulting deck.

Salesperson: Honest question: I have 20 active opportunities. If I build a Deal Plan for each one, I won't have time left to actually sell.

RSM: Good. Then don't.

You don't do this depth for 20 deals. You do it for five with the biggest revenue and highest strategic value. Remember:

"Understanding needs is insight; turning them into aligned action is mastery."

Mastery is expensive. You don't spend it on everyone.

Salesperson: And addressing those needs is "all about preparation," right?

RSM: Exactly. The real work happens inside your own company. You sit with your engineering and ask: "How can we address their concerns about implementation?" You talk to product marketing and ask them: "When you speak with their CTO, please share the roadmap addressing AI integration."

You sit with me and the VP of Sales to get our feedback on the pricing and payment terms. We will have to understand why we have to discount the just-released product.

Salesperson: Yes. It is the way. Yesterday, I learned to touch Inspiration without sounding fake. Today, I learned about Motivation—the waves and suppressed needs.

RSM: Exactly. You used to think a deal is won with "a strong pitch." Now you know: The deal is won in the stories your advocates tell when you're not in the room. Your job is to design those.

(*He turns the notebook around so the Salesperson can read the table.*)

RSM: Homework:
  Pick one big deal.
  List the top 5–7 stakeholders.
  For each:
  Expressed needs
  Your best guess at suppressed needs
  One message
  One messenger.

Bring it tomorrow. Then we'll talk about the last layer: Persuasion—how to make "yes" feel better than "do nothing."

Salesperson: Goals, purpose, suppressed needs, deal plans, messengers, timing... You know, this is starting to feel less like selling and more like... a strategy computer game.

RSM: Exactly. You're not just running deals. You're playing a strategy game against your competitors.

Scene 4: Persuasion, The Choreography of Yes

The next evening. The office is nearly silent, with only the hum of the HVAC breaking the stillness. The Deal Plan for the InTECH account sits in the center of the table, filled out in the Salesperson's messy handwriting. The Salesperson looks at it, pleased but restless. He taps his pen against the paper.

Salesperson: Okay. I did the homework. I mapped the stakeholders. I know the Product Owner is terrified of burnout. His suppressed need is Safety.

I know the COO is desperate to look like an innovator, masking his Esteem in the meetings. I know what to tell them. So... I just book the meeting, show them this plan, and we're good?

(*RSM laughs softly*)

RSM: If you walk in and "just show" them the plan, you lose.

Salesperson: Why? I have the psychological map! You said this was the hard part.

RSM: No. This was the diagnostic part. Knowing a patient has a broken leg is diagnosis. Setting the bone without causing them to scream is surgery. You are about to walk into a room of irrational, stressed, cognitive-biased brains. If you just dump raw logic on them, they will freeze.

You need Persuasion.

And as we discussed in Chapter 3, Persuasion isn't magic. It is choreography.

Salesperson: Choreography. Great. Now I need dancing shoes.

RSM: You need a sequence.

(RSM *slides a clean sheet of paper over.*)

You are going to take this Deal Plan and run it through the Five Stages:

Connect → Frame → Solve → Vision → Commit.

And at every stage, you will use a Heuristic—a mental shortcut—to make the decision easy for their brains to process.

Salesperson: Walk me through it. Live. I'm meeting the insecure COO next Tuesday. He wants to look like an innovator, but he's insecure because he doesn't understand the tech.

RSM: Stage 1: Connect.

How do you start? Do you launch into your bio and the agenda?

Salesperson: Usually? Yes. It shows I'm professional.

RSM: It shows you are cold. He is already on edge. If you start with a formal agenda, he puts his guard up.

Use the Halo Effect:

Walk in with warmth, calm, and total presence. If the first minute feels safe, his brain assumes your product is also safe.

Then, use Reciprocal Self-Disclosure:

Don't just ask him about his pain. Share a small struggle of your own first. "You know, looking at your integration challenge, I was reminded of a project I struggled with last year. We had the exact same bottleneck, and it kept me up at night..."

When you open up, he feels safe to admit he doesn't know the answer.

Salesperson: Okay. I create a warm halo, I share a struggle, he relaxes.

Then should I show the solution?

RSM: No! You haven't framed the problem yet.

Stage 2: Frame.

If you just show the solution now, it looks like an expense.

You need to change how he names his reality. Use Narrative Relabeling. Don't call his current setup "The existing system."

Call it "Legacy Debt."

Salesperson: "Legacy Debt"? Seriously? If I walk in there and call his architecture "debt," he's going to kick me out. It sounds like I'm insulting his work.

RSM: You aren't insulting him. You're naming the enemy that keeps him up at night. Think about it. If you call it "The Current System," how does that feel?

Salesperson: Neutral. Safe.

RSM: Exactly. "System" implies stability. It implies you can keep it forever. But "Debt"? Debt implies interest. Debt compounds. Debt means every day he waits, the price goes up. His brain knows debt must be paid before it kills him. You are not calling him a failure. You are labeling the situation as a trap he needs to escape. Salesperson: So I'm moving him from "comfortable" to "urgent" just by changing the label.

RSM: Yes. And then, you reframe his reality with Anchoring. "Most market leaders in your sector are cutting this debt by 20% this year to stay competitive. Where is your team relative to that?" Now he isn't just listening; he is measuring himself against a standard you set.

Salesperson: That's... intense. But I see why it works.

Now that he sees the "Debt," I move to Stage 3: Solve.

How do I present the fix?

RSM: I know you. You love to show the 50-slide roadmap. If you do that, he will tune it out because he doesn't understand the tech. Instead, use the IKEA Effect.

Stop bringing the "Perfect Timeline" slide. Bring a slide with empty boxes for Q3 and Q4. Ask him: "Given your team's load, which month looks realistic for the pilot?"

Salesperson: Will that work? Just asking him to fill in a box?

RSM: It works because you aren't dictating the schedule—he is. When he looks at that empty box and says "October," he suddenly owns October. You type it in, but *he* built it. He will defend that date to his own board because it was his choice. That is the IKEA Effect. We love what we build.

Salesperson: Yes, he probably will stick to that.

RSM: To make the solution safe, back it up with Authority Bias. "This is the same deployment cadence we used with Meta and Google. This slide shows the industry benchmark from IoT Authority; we deliver 27% improvement to our customers."

Salesperson: Okay. He built the plan with me. He feels safe. Should I ask for the signature?

RSM: Not yet. He hasn't felt the future yet.

Stage 4: *Vision*.

You need to help him see the future. He needs to imagine himself benefiting from the solution. To see himself succeed. At the same time, you may help him envision what will happen if he does not implement our solution. Both positive and negative.

Use Anticipated Regret. Ask him:

"If we pause this now, and the board asks in six months why the 'Legacy Debt' is still slowing down product launches, what will we tell them?"

Make him visualize the conversation where he must explain failure. Then, give him a Label to live up to.

"You're the one turning this ship around. You're the Change Agent here."

Salesperson: Nice. I like it. He is the hero.

RSM: Precisely. You've given him the identity of a hero. But even heroes get cold feet when they stare at a three-year contract. That brings us to the final hurdle.

Stage 5: *Commit*.

Your mistake here is usually asking for a huge, terrifying decision that feels like a cliff edge. You need to lower the barrier.

Use Hyperbolic Discounting:

Human brains value a small reward now much more than a huge reward in three years. So, don't sell him the 3-year ROI. Sell him the "Quick Win." "If we sign this week, we can clean up the reporting dashboard before your next board meeting." Give him a reward he can touch now.

Salesperson: That connects back to his Esteem again—he looks good immediately. And then I just hope he signs?

RSM: Hope is not a strategy. You lock it in with If-Then Planning and a touch of Scarcity. You need to tie the timeline to a specific consequence. Try this:

"If we get legal approvals by the 1st, then we sign on the 5th. If we hit that date, I can lock in the implementation team for the 15th. But if we miss it, that team is booked on a parallel project for Q3, so we'd be looking at some delays in getting those results to your board."

You are trading the signature for a guaranteed resource. Yet, if he does not decide quickly, he will lose time. That is the Scarcity Heuristic.

(Salesperson Leans back, exhaling slowly)

Salesperson: Wow. It's not just "asking for the order." It's a complete narrative arc:

Connect with warmth and disclosure. Frame the current state using labels like "Debt." Solve by letting him build the plan (IKEA). Vision by making him fear regret and seeing himself winning. Commit by creating scarcity and a concrete deadline.

RSM: *(Standing up)* That is Persuasion. It is not luck. It is architecture.

(The RSM picks up his jacket from the back of the chair and puts it on. He straightens his collar, looking at the Salesperson one last time.)

RSM: You have the Inspiration—you know Why they exist.

You have the Motivation—you know What they secretly need.

You have the Persuasion—you know How to guide the decision.

(The Salesperson looks down at the Deal Plan, then up at the RSM. His cynicism is gone. He looks steady. Ready.)

Salesperson: Yes. I can do this.

(The RSM nods and walks toward the closed door. He puts his hand on the handle, then stops. He turns back, a faint smile playing on his lips.)

RSM: One last thing. Have you noticed what just happened in this room?

Salesperson: What do you mean? You coached me.

RSM: No. I Persuaded you.

Salesperson: *(Frowns)* Excuse me?

RSM: Think about the last few days:

Step 1, Connect: I didn't start by lecturing you. I sat in the dark with you and listened to your pain about the lost Meridian deal. I used Reciprocal Self-Disclosure to show I knew how it felt.

Step 2, Frame: I didn't say you were a "bad salesperson." I used Reframing. I showed you that you were "doing everything right" but missing the hidden layer. I changed your map of reality.

Step 3, Solve: I didn't give you vague advice. I gave you a specific tool—the Deal Plan—and let you fill it out yourself. That was the IKEA Effect.

Step 4, Vision: I made you Visualize exactly who to talk to and what to say, until you could see the win. You see yourself using the tools and winning deals.

Step 5, Commit: I gave you homework. Small, specific steps. Foot-in-the-Door.

(The RSM leans against the doorframe.)

RSM: I didn't just teach you architecture. I used it.

And now, you are ready to act.

(He stares at him, then looks at the notes on the table. A slow realization spreads across his face.)

Salesperson: You used the flow on me.

RSM: It works on CEOs. It works on toddlers. And apparently, it works with cynical salespeople.

(He opens the door and steps out into the hallway, pausing just before he leaves.)

RSM: Now go use it on someone who pays us.

(The door clicks shut. The Salesperson is left alone in the quiet room. He looks at the "Persuasion" list on his notepad, then circles it twice. He picks up the phone.)

Epilogue

Dear Reader,

For as long as I can remember, I have searched for the "code" behind human behavior. When I was young, I looked for a single book that would grant me the practical wisdom to drive decisions and persuade people.

I asked everyone: my parents, psychologists, doctors, teachers, and even veterans of intelligence units. Yet no one could point to a single framework that effectively explained how to drive human decisions. At eighteen, when I began my engineering degree, I paused my search to focus on mathematics and electronics.

But the fire never went out. I was still hunting for a unified theory of human drive.

Many years later, in 2020, as the world locked down due to the COVID-19 pandemic, I wrote my first book, *Sellosophy*. I wanted to see if the timeless questions of philosophy could survive the brutal scrutiny of a sales floor.

In my early writing, I attempted to reconcile two seemingly contradictory theories: Abraham Maslow's hierarchy of needs, which states that self-actualization can only occur after basic needs are met, and Viktor Frankl's experience in the concentration camps, which demonstrated that striving for a meaning bigger than ourselves is the true path to self-actualization and happiness.

Back then, I couldn't fully solve the puzzle. I merely planted a seed, stating that a drive born of belief (Inspiration) is stronger than a drive born of human needs (Motivation). But I knew I didn't have the full picture. I kept searching.

It took me five more years of meditation, reading, and field experience to settle this contradiction. That synthesis is the foundation of this book, *Sellchology*.

I realized I could not neglect the modern findings of behavioral psychology from giants like Daniel Kahneman, Amos Tversky, Charlie Munger, Robert Cialdini, and Dan Ariely. Their research proved that people can be influenced to take irrational actions that are inconsistent with their stated needs or goals. The more I read and the more I practiced my craft, the more I realized that all of them were right. Maslow, Frankl, and Kahneman each stood the test of time.

My conclusion was simple: we humans are complex.

Therefore, combining all three theories creates maximum drive. I took this hypothesis into the ultimate psychology lab: high-stakes B2B sales negotiations. In our world, orders and bookings are the indisputable truth, proving or disproving any theory.

Commissions are paid only on reality.

This experience led me to write this book—an integration of these theories for the practical world of sales.

To navigate the day-to-day hustle, I use the analogy of The River of Decision to remember how Inspiration, Motivation, and Persuasion combine to generate the maximum customer drive.

Figure: The River of Decision[113]

In the illustration above, we see a river streaming through a natural terrain. Each element in this picture illustrates a specific Drive and how they combine.

The Sea: Gravity pulls the water relentlessly toward the vast sea—just as **Inspiration** pulls the soul. This is the "Meaning," the "Why." It is the invisible force that pulls the water together into a strong river, giving it direction and purpose.

The Terrain: The mountains, valleys, and forests represent **Motivation**. This is how the river finds its path to the sea. The water cannot simply fly over the mountains; it must navigate the reality of the terrain. It widens in the valleys and narrows as it passes through the hills. This mirrors human needs. Just as the water must obey the landscape, humans must satisfy their needs. In many cases, humans—like the river—lose sight of the sea. They become focused solely on getting around the next hill or surviving the forest.

The Current: The dynamic stream of the water represents **Persuasion.** Water acts in complex ways. It may seep into the soil and remain trapped in underground lakes for decades. Yet, under pressure, it may burst out of a rock, creating a spring. With enough pressure and velocity, strong currents can carve through rock—just as the right Persuasion can move humans to act against even their most stubborn needs.

To have the maximum impact, we cannot rely on just one force. We must utilize all three:

The Sea is the Inspiration of Frankl.

The Terrain is the Motivation of Maslow.

The Current is the Persuasion of Kahneman.

Just as the river needs all three to reach the ocean, we must use Inspiration, Motivation, and Persuasion to guide our customers toward the final decision.

Because I could not find a book that would satisfy my search for a unified theory of human drive, I wrote it myself.

Now, I can finally repay the debt to my younger self. I can look back at that 18-year-old student and say:

"I found the book."

It is called *Sellchology.*

Final Words

Thank you for taking this journey with me.

I hope you found what you were looking for. As we have discussed, the human mind is not built to retain endless lists or dry facts. After a few weeks, the specific frameworks may fade. That is perfectly okay. That is simply how we are wired: for stories, symbols, and patterns. My hope is not that you memorize every page, but that you permanently shift how you see the humans across the table.

To bridge the gap between reading and doing, I have included short summaries at the end of each chapter. Treat them as your tactical guides—anchors for when the pace of a deal accelerates.

Our dialogue does not end with this page. I look forward to hearing your stories from the trenches.

I wish you the very best.

Ariel Feder

Sellosophy.ariel@gmail.com

About the Author

Ariel Feder began his career as a Captain in the Communication Corps, designing complex radio systems. He soon realized, however, that the most complex systems weren't found on circuit boards—they were in the boardroom.

Having transitioned from engineering to sales leadership, Ariel has spent two decades mastering the "soft" psychological dynamics of the "hard" technology sector.

Working with startups and global companies across the Israeli high-tech industry, he has decoded the human patterns that drive high-stakes deals. Today, he approaches sales with an engineer's mind, blending philosophy, psychology, and street smarts into practical models.

Ariel is the author of *Sellosophy* and his latest release, *Sellchology*. Together, his works offer a comprehensive, field-tested framework for mastering sales management and sales psychology.

He holds a B.Sc. in Electronic Engineering and an MBA in Business and Finance, and he has completed executive education at Harvard Business School.

Endnotes

1   Isaac Newton, letter to Robert Hooke, February 5, 1676, in The Correspondence of Isaac Newton, vol. 1, ed. H. W. Turnbull (Cambridge University Press, 1959), 416.

2   Friedrich Nietzsche, "Maxims and Arrows," in Twilight of the Idols, trans. R. J. Hollingdale (Penguin Books, 1968), 33.

3   Genesis 2:7 (King James Version).

4   Deuteronomy 6:4 (The Jewish Publication Society, 1962).

5   Talmud Bavli, Berakhot 61b, trans. Isidore Epstein (Soncino Press, 1938)

6   Andrew George, trans., The Epic of Gilgamesh (Penguin Classics, 2003), Tablet IX, 70.

7   N. K. Sandars, trans., The Epic of Gilgamesh (Penguin Classics,1972), Prologue/Tablet XI, 117

8   Yuval Noah Harari, Sapiens: A Brief History of Humankind (Harper, 2015), 25.

9   Friedrich Nietzsche, "Maxims and Arrows," in Twilight of the Idols, trans. R. J. Hollingdale (Penguin Books, 1968), 33.

10 Viktor Frankl Institute, "Life and Work," accessed January 29,2026, viktorfranklinstitute.org/biography.

11 Viktor E. Frankl, Man's Search for Meaning (Beacon Press, 2006), 111.

12 Viktor E. Frankl, Man's Search for Meaning (Beacon Press, 2006), 109.

13 Viktor E. Frankl, Man's Search for Meaning (Beacon Press, 2006), 16

14 Edward Hoffman, The Right to Be Human: A Biography of Abraham Maslow (Jeremy P. Tarcher, Inc., 1988), 5.

15 Edward Hoffman, The Right to Be Human: A Biography of Abraham Maslow (Jeremy P. Tarcher, Inc., 1988), 8.

16 Edward Hoffman, The Right to Be Human: A Biography of Abraham Maslow (Jeremy P. Tarcher, Inc., 1988), 24–25.

17 Edward Hoffman, The Right to Be Human: A Biography of Abraham Maslow (Jeremy P. Tarcher, Inc., 1988), 113.

18 Abraham H. Maslow, "A Theory of Human Motivation," Psychological Review 50, no. 4 (1943): 370–396

19 Emmanuel-Auguste-Dieudonné, Count de Las Cases, Journal of the Private Life and Conversations of the Emperor Napoleon at Saint Helena (London: Henry Colburn, 1824), Vol. 4

20   Thomas Hobbes, Leviathan (1651), Part I, Chapter XIII: "Of the Natural Condition of Mankind as Concerning Their Felicity and Misery."

21   Epicurus, Principal Doctrines, Maxim 27. This collection of forty essential teachings was preserved by the third-century historian Diogenes Laërtius in his work Lives of Eminent Philosophers (Book X)

22   Alfred Adler, Understanding Human Nature (New York: Greenberg, 1927)

23   The Dhammapada: The Buddha's Path of Wisdom, trans. Acharya Buddharakkhita (Buddhist Publication Society, 1985), verse 166.

24   Abraham H. Maslow, "A Theory of Human Motivation," Psychological Review 50, no. 4 (1943): 370–396.

25   David Krech, Richard S. Crutchfield and Egerton L. Ballachey, Individual in Society: A Textbook of Social Psychology (McGraw-Hill Kogakusha, 1962).

26   David Krech, Richard S. Crutchfield, and Egerton L. Ballachey, Individual in Society: A Textbook of Social Psychology (McGraw-Hill Kogakusha, 1962), 77

27   Walter Isaacson, Einstein: His Life and Universe (Simon & Schuster, 2007)

28   Maslow, Abraham H. Motivation and Personality. New York, Harper & Brothers, 1954. p. 97

29   Abraham H. Maslow, Toward a Psychology of Being (D. Van Nostrand Company, 1962).

30   Clive Staples Lewis, Mere Christianity (Geoffrey Bles, 1952), book IV, chap. 11, "The New Men."

31   Chris Voss and Tahl Raz, Never Split the Difference: Negotiating As If Your Life Depended On It (Harper Business, 2016), chap. 7.

32   Spencer Johnson, Who Moved My Cheese? An Amazing Way to Deal with Change in Your Work and in Your Life (G. P. Putnam's Sons, 1998).

33   V. L. Smith and H. H. Clark, "On the Uses and Meanings of Rising Declaratives," Language 87, no. 3 (2011): 529–565.

34   WayWithWords, "Training AI for Call Analytics: The Role of Quality Speech Data," October 14, 2025, waywithwords.net.

35   D. Keltner and G. A. Bonanno, "A Study of Laughter and Dissociation: Distinct Correlates of Laughter and Smiling During Bereavement," Journal of Personality and Social Psychology 73, no. 4 (1997): 687–702.

36   SalesTech Star, "Neuroadaptive Salestech and AI: Reading Human Cues in Real-time," October 20, 2025, salestechstar.com

37   G. Rennie, O. Perepelkina, and A. Vinciarelli, "Which Model is Best: Comparing Methods and Metrics for Automatic Laughter Detection," Interspeech 2022 (2022): 4008–4012.

38   D. Keltner and G. A. Bonanno, "A Study of Laughter and Dissociation: Distinct Correlates of Laughter and Smiling During Bereavement,"

Journal of Personality and Social Psychology 73, no. 4 (1997): 687–702

39   WayWithWords, "The Role of Acoustic Sentiment in Sales AI," June 9, 2025, waywithwords.net

40   M. Heldner, On the Timing of Turn-Taking in Human Interaction (Stockholm University Press, 2023)

41   Search Engine Journal, "How Gong and Uniphore Use AI to Detect Suppressed Objections in Real-Time," November 12, 2025.

42   R. Dendukuri et al., "Uncharacteristic Delays as Indicators of Cognitive Load in Conversational AI," Journal of Linguistic Research (2021)

43   P. O'Connor, Y. Zhang, and P. Falk, "Conversational Patterns: Identifying Topic Recurrence in Sales Dialogue," Journal of Communication Analytics 15, no. 1 (2022): 33–50.

44   Smith Insights, "Emotion-Aware AI in Sales: Frequency of Topic Revisitations as Predictors of Objections," 2024, smithinsights.ai.

45   Heraclitus, Fragment DK 22 B 67a, in Die Fragmente der Vorsokratiker, vol. 1, eds. H. Diels and W. Kranz (Weidmann, 1951).

46   Jihun Hamm et al., "Automated Facial Action Coding System for Dynamic Analysis of Facial Expressions in Neuropsychiatric Disorders," Journal of Neuroscience Methods 200, no. 2 (2011): 237–256.

47   Hang Li, Su-Jing Wang, and Weihong Deng, "Deep MicroExpression Recognition: A Survey," IEEE Transactions on Affective Computing (2023).

48   Lei Zhang et al., "Spatiotemporal Transformer for MicroExpression Recognition in the Wild," Proceedings of the AAAI Conference on Artificial Intelligence (2024).

49   Joe Navarro and Marvin Karlins, What Every Body Is Saying: An ExFBI Agent's Guide to Speed-Reading People (HarperCollins, 2008).

50   Bella M. DePaulo et al., "Cues to Deception," Psychological Bulletin 129, no. 1 (2003): 74–118.

51   Paul Ekman and Wallace V. Friesen, "Nonverbal Leakage and Clues to Deception," Psychiatry 32, no. 1 (1969): 88–106.

52   Aldert Vrij and Pär Anders Granhag, "Interviewing to Detect Deception," in The Handbook of Eyewitness Psychology, vol. 1, eds. Michael P. Toglia et al. (Lawrence Erlbaum Associates, 2007), 267– 291.

53   Tanya L. Chartrand and John A. Bargh, "The Chameleon Effect: The Perception-Behavior Link and Social Interaction," Journal of Personality and Social Psychology 76, no. 6 (1999): 893–910.

54   Jessica L. Lakin et al., "The Chameleon Effect as Social Glue: Evidence for the Evolutionary Significance of Nonconscious Mimicry," Journal of Nonverbal Behavior 27, no. 3 (2003): 145–162.

55   Sybill.ai, "AI Behavioral Analytics: Mirroring, Rapport, and Deal Outcomes,"

2024, sybill.ai.

56   Gartner, "New B2B Buying Journey & its Implication for Sales," Gartner Sales Practice (2019)

57   Matthew Dixon and Brent Adamson, The Challenger Sale: Taking Control of the Customer Conversation (Penguin Portfolio, 2011), 46.

58   Brent Adamson, "Sense Making for Sales: How High-Performing Sellers Help Customers Make Better Decisions," Gartner for Sales Leaders (2020)

59   Chris Voss and Tahl Raz, Never Split the Difference: Negotiating As If Your Life Depended On It (Harper Business, 2016).

60   Carl R. Rogers, On Becoming a Person: A Therapist's View of Psychotherapy (Houghton Mifflin, 1961).

61   Dale Carnegie, How to Win Friends and Influence People (Simon & Schuster, 1936).

62   Jean Piaget, The Origins of Intelligence in Children (International Universities Press, 1952).

63   Thomas S. Kuhn, The Structure of Scientific Revolutions (University of Chicago Press, 1962).

64   Spencer Johnson, Who Moved My Cheese? An Amazing Way to Deal with Change in Your Work and in Your Life (Putnam, 1998).

65   Viktor E. Frankl, Man's Search for Meaning (Beacon Press, 2006).

66   Clayton M. Christensen et al., Competing Against Luck: The Story of Innovation and Customer Choice (Harper Business, 2016).

67   Barry Schwartz, The Paradox of Choice: Why More Is Less (Ecco, 2004).

68   Peter Block, Flawless Consulting: A Guide to Getting Your Expertise Used, 3rd ed. (Pfeiffer, 2011).

69   William James, The Principles of Psychology (1890).

70   John Dewey, Human Nature and Conduct: An Introduction to Social Psychology (Henry Holt and Company, 1922).

71   Laozi, Tao Te Ching, trans. D. C. Lau (Penguin Classics, 1963).

72   Aristotle, Nicomachean Ethics, trans. Roger Crisp (Cambridge University Press, 2000).

73   Aristotle, Nicomachean Ethics, book VII, chaps. 1–10

74   Daniel Kahneman and Amos Tversky, "Prospect Theory: An Analysis of Decision under Risk," Econometrica 47, no. 2 (1979): 263–291.

75   Amos Tversky and Daniel Kahneman, "Judgment under Uncertainty: Heuristics and Biases," Science 185, no. 4157 (1974): 1124–1131

76   William Samuelson and Richard Zeckhauser, "Status Quo Bias inDecision Making," Journal of Risk and Uncertainty 1, no. 1 (1988): 7–59.

77   Daniel Kahneman, Thinking, Fast and Slow (Farrar, Straus and Giroux, 2011).

78   Zig Ziglar, Secrets of Closing the Sale (Fleming H. Revell Company,1984).

79   Tom Hopkins, How to Master the Art of Selling (Warner Books, 1980).

80   Richard E. Nisbett and Timothy D. Wilson, "The Halo Effect: Evidence for Unconscious Alteration of Judgments," Journal of Personality and Social Psychology 35, no. 4 (1977): 250–256.

81   Robert B. Cialdini, Influence: Science and Practice, 4th ed. (Allyn & Bacon, 2001).

82   Marilynn B. Brewer, "The Psychology of Prejudice: Ingroup Love and Outgroup Hate," Journal of Social Issues 55, no. 3 (1999): 429– 444

83   Nancy L. Collins and Lynn C. Miller, "Self-Disclosure and Liking: A Meta-Analytic Review," Psychological Bulletin 116, no. 3 (1994): 457–475

84   Thomas Gilovich, Dale Griffin, and Daniel Kahneman, eds., Heuristics and Biases: The Psychology of Intuitive Judgment (Cambridge University Press, 2002), 397–420

85   Theodore Roosevelt, Theodore Roosevelt: An Autobiography (Macmillan, 1910).

86   Theodor Herzl, Altneuland (Old New Land) (Seemann Nachfolger, 1902).

87   Amos Tversky and Daniel Kahneman, "Judgment under Uncertainty: Heuristics and Biases," Science 185, no. 4157 (1974): 1124–1131.

88   Valerio Capraro and Andrea Vanzo, "The Power of Moral Words: Loaded Language Generates Framing Effects in the Extreme Dictator Game," Economics Letters 185 (2019): 108718.

89   Jerry Suls and Choi K. Wan, "In Search of the False-Uniqueness Phenomenon: Fear and Estimates of Social Consensus," Journal of Personality and Social Psychology 52, no. 2 (1987): 211–217.

90   Amos Tversky and Daniel Kahneman, "The Framing of Decisions and the Psychology of Choice," Science 211, no. 4481 (1981): 453–458

91   Nassim Nicholas Taleb, The Black Swan: The Impact of the Highly Improbable (Random House, 2007).

92   Charles F. Kettering, Prophet of Progress: Selections from the Speeches of Charles F. Kettering (E. P. Dutton, 1949).

93   Stanley Milgram, Obedience to Authority: An Experimental View. New York: Harper & Row, 1974.

94   Charles T. Munger, Poor Charlie's Almanack: The Wit and Wisdom of Charles T. Munger (Walsworth Publishing Company, 2005)

95   Daniel Kahneman and Amos Tversky, "Prospect Theory: An Analysis of

Decision under Risk," Econometrica 47, no. 2 (1979): 263–291.

96   Barry Schwartz, The Paradox of Choice: Why More Is Less (Harper Perennial, 2004)

97   Rolf Reber, Norbert Schwarz, and Piotr Winkielman, "Processing Fluency and Aesthetic Pleasure: Is Beauty in the Perceiver's Processing Experience?" Personality and Social Psychology Review 8, no. 4 (2004): 364–382.

98   Michael I. Norton, Daniel Mochon, and Dan Ariely, "The IKEA Effect: When Labor Leads to Love," Journal of Consumer Psychology 22, no. 3 (2012): 453–460.

99   Albert Einstein, On the Method of Theoretical Physics (Oxford University Press, 1933).

100   Lien B. Pham and Shelley E. Taylor, "From Thought to Action: Effects of Process-Versus Outcome-Based Mental Simulations on Performance," Personality and Social Psychology Bulletin 25, no. 2 (1999): 250–260

101   Ran Kivetz, Oleg Urminsky, and Yuhuang Zheng, "The GoalGradient Hypothesis Resurrected: Purchase Acceleration, Illusionary Goal Progress, and Customer Retention," Journal of Marketing Research 43, no. 1 (2006): 39–58

102   Daryl J. Bem, "Self-Perception Theory," in Advances in Experimental Social Psychology, vol. 6, ed. Leonard Berkowitz (Academic Press, 1972), 1–62.

103   Hal R. Arkes and Catherine Blumer, "The Psychology of Sunk Cost," Organizational Behavior and Human Decision Processes 35, no. 1 (1985): 124–140

104   Graham Loomes and Robert Sugden, "Regret Theory: An Alternative Theory of Rational Choice under Uncertainty," The Economic Journal 92, no. 368 (1982): 805–824.

105   Napoleon Hill, Think and Grow Rich (The Ralston Society, 1937)

106   Stephen Worchel, Jerry Lee, and Akanbi Adewole, "Effects of Supply and Demand on Ratings of Object Value," Journal of Personality and Social Psychology 32, no. 5 (1975): 906–914

107   George Ainslie, "Specious Reward: A Behavioral Theory of Impulsiveness and Impulse Control," Psychological Bulletin 82, no. 4 (1975): 463–496.

108   Jonathan L. Freedman and Scott C. Fraser, "Compliance without Pressure: The Foot-in-the-Door Technique," Journal of Personality and Social Psychology 4, no. 2 (1966): 195–202

109   Barry M. Staw, "Knee-Deep in the Big Muddy: A Study of Escalating Commitment to a Chosen Course of Action," Organizational Behavior and Human Performance 16, no. 1 (1976): 27–44

110 Peter M. Gollwitzer, "Implementation Intentions: Strong Effects of Simple Plans," American Psychologist 54, no. 7 (1999): 493–503.

111 Glengarry Glen Ross, directed by James Foley (New Line Cinema, 1992).

112 Jacques Abbadie, Traité de la Vérité de la Religion Chrétienne (Reinier Leers, 1684), chap. 2.

113 Figure 5.1: The River of Decision. Visual illustration created with the assistance of AI, based on the author's original sketches.

www.ingramcontent.com/pod-product-compliance
Lightning Source LLC
Chambersburg PA
CBHW020923160726
47993CB00005B/2106